After the Crash: Recession or Depression?

Also by A. Gary Shilling

IS INFLATION ENDING? ARE YOU READY?

(Co-authored with Kiril
Sokoloff, McGraw-Hill, 1983)

THE WORLD HAS DEFINITELY CHANGED:
NEW ECONOMIC FORCES AND THEIR IMPLICATIONS
FOR THE NEXT DECADE

(Lakeview Press, 1986)

After the Crash: Recession or Depression?

Business and Investment Strategies for a Deflationary World

A. Gary Shilling

Lakeview Economic Services

First Edition -- March 1988

Library of Congress Card Number 88-080480

Published by Lakeview Economic Services
P.O. Box 521
Short Hills, NJ   07078

Cover art by The Warbler Group

Printed by Offset Paperback Mfrs., Inc.
Dallas, Pennsylvania   18612

To my wife, Peggy,
for supporting, encouraging,
and putting up with me for 25 years

Contents

viii

About the Author

Dr. A. Gary Shilling is President of A. Gary Shilling &
Company, Inc., economic consultants to a number of
leading financial institutions and industrial corporations,
registered investment advisors, and member of the New
York Stock Exchange. The firm also publishes inSight, a
monthly report of economic forecasts and investment
strategy. Dr. Shilling is also general partner of Thematic
Investment Partners, an investment partnership oriented
toward long-term economic themes.

He received his A.B. degree in physics, magna cum
laude, from Amherst College where he was also elected to
Phi Beta Kappa and Sigma Xi. Dr. Shilling earned his
M.A. and Ph.D. in economics at Stanford University.
While on the West Coast he served on the staffs of the
Federal Reserve Bank of San Francisco and the Bank of
America.

Before establishing his own firm in 1978, Dr. Shilling
was Senior Vice President and Chief Economist of White,
Weld & Co., Inc. Earlier his experience included setting
up the Economics Department at Merrill Lynch, Pierce,
Fenner & Smith at age 29 and serving as the firm's first
chief economist. Prior to Merrill Lynch, he was with
Standard Oil Co. (N.J.) where he was in charge of U.S. and
Canadian economic analysis and forecasting.

Dr. Shilling has published numerous articles on the
business outlook and techniques of economic analysis and
forecasting, and he serves as Associate Editor of Business
Economics, the journal of the National Association of
Business Economists. His first book, Is Inflation Ending?

Are You Ready?, co-authored with Kiril Sokoloff, was published by McGraw-Hill early in 1983. The World Has Definitely Changed: New Economic Forces and Their Implications for the Next Decade, was published late in 1986.

Dr. Shilling is well known for his forecasting record. In the spring of 1969 he was among the few who correctly forecast that a recession would start late in the year. In early 1973 he stood almost alone in forecasting that the world was entering a massive inventory building spree to be followed by the first major worldwide recession since the 1930s. In the late 1970s when most thought that raging inflation would last forever, he was the first to predict that the changing political mood of the country would lead to an end of severe inflation, as well as to potentially serious financial and economic readjustment problems, and a shift in successful investment strategy from one favoring tangibles to emphasis on stocks and bonds. Subsequently, he has become known as "Doctor Disinflation."

The January 5, 1987 edition of The Wall Street Journal said, "According to the average estimate of 25 economists surveyed by The Wall Street Journal a year ago, the 30-year Treasury bond yield would rise to 9.76% by Dec. 31, 1986, from 9.27% at the end of 1985. That prediction turned out to be more than 2 1/4 percentage points too high. The best estimate came from Mr. Shilling, who said 8%."

Six months earlier, the June 30 , 1986 edition of the Journal stated: "Mr. Shilling's interest-rate forecasts of six months ago proved to be very close to the mark. He had expected a 6% rate on three-month Treasury bills and an 8% yield on 30-year Treasury bonds by the middle of this year. Those were by far the closest of the 25 analysts polled last December."

On January 2, 1986, The Wall Street Journal stated: "One year ago, 23 of the 24 economists in this newspaper's survey predicted that the yield on 30-year Treasury bonds, then 11.53%, would close 1985 in double digits. Instead, the bond closed Tuesday [December 31, 1985] at 9.27%. . . . The only forecaster who had expected a single-digit yield was A. Gary Shilling. . ."

Twice a poll of financial institutions conducted by the Institutional Investor magazine ranked Dr. Shilling as Wall Street's top economist.

A frequent contributor to the financial press, his articles appear in The Wall Street Journal and Forbes magazine, among others, and he is a regular columnist for the Los Angeles Times and a member of its Board of Economists. Dr. Shilling is also a member of The Nihon Keizai Shimbun (Japan Economic Journal) Board of Economists. He has been a guest on such television programs as MacNeil/Lehrer News Hour, Wall Street Week and the Merv Griffin Show. Recognized as an effective and dynamic speaker, he often addresses national and international conventions of various business groups including the Conference Board and the Young Presidents' Organization.

Dr. Shilling is on the Board of Directors of Aim Packaging, Inc., the Henry H. Kessler Foundation, Inc., the Episcopal Evangelism Foundation, and the Parents Council of Bucknell University; Co-Chairman of the Parents Fund Committee of Bates College; a Trustee of Kent Place School, and the New Jersey Shakespeare Festival; and founder of the Episcopal Church Excellence in Preaching Program. He was a member of the National Commission on Jobs and Small Business. He served as economic advisor to George Bush in his 1980 presidential campaign, a consultant to the Reagan-Bush '84 campaign, and is an informal adviser to the Reagan Administration. He has testified before various Congressional Committees including the Joint Economic Committee and the House Banking Committee.

Index of Figures

Preface

The stock market crash of October 1987 has convinced many in and out of Wall Street that the world has definitely changed. Gone is the implicit or explicit conviction that money can be made easily in securities and with little risk.

Quite the opposite. The 1987 Crash focused attention on the 1929 Crash and raised some disturbing questions. Did it merely blow away the speculative fluff that had accumulated in the preceding year and leave stock prices where they were in late 1986, or was it, like the 1929 collapse in stock prices, a prelude to financial and economic calamity as well?

These questions are even more disturbing to those who recognize that now, like in 1929, there are tremendous imbalances in the world. Foreign trade imbalances among industrialized countries are extreme. Growing protectionism is a major threat to global trade and economic expansion. Third World debt problems are nearly hopeless. Japan appears to be on the brink of major financial problems and a possible economic depression. The U.S. has been the only major source of world demand in the last five years; has financed that demand through unprecedented borrowing by the federal government, business, and consumers; and transmitted it to the rest of the world by a skyrocketing trade deficit. Moreover, Washington has virtually run out of policy options to deal with any financial crises or economic decline the Crash may have foreshadowed, whether through dollar manipulation, monetary policy changes, or fiscal stimulation or contraction.

In many ways, events are right on the schedule that we spelled out in the fall of 1986 in our book, The World Has Definitely Changed: New Economic Forces and Their Implications for the Next Decade. Chapter 24, "Depression Is More Likely Than Many May Think," listed the many disturbing parallels between the world in 1986 and that of the late 1920s. It also pointed out that all the safeguards introduced in the 1930s to prevent another stock market crash had been superseded by stock options, futures contracts, junk bonds, and program trading.

Furthermore, as predicted in that book, international competition continues to be fierce despite the ongoing slide in the dollar. Cost control has become the new corporate creed. The purchasing power of middle-income households continues to be squeezed. Serious inflation has not reoccurred despite the weak dollar. Protectionism and global financial problems are greater threats than they appeared to be in the fall of 1986.

Still, enough new factors of long-term significance have developed in the last 18 months, some of them through evolution and some of them completely new (at least to us), to warrant a sequel to The World Has Definitely Changed. This book is that sequel, not a revision of the earlier work which still seems relevant and useful.

Consequently, both books should be read to capture the full scope of how we think the world has changed and its implications. The introduction to this book is a brief summary of that earlier one -- a refresher for those who read it, and a spur for those who haven't read it to do so now.

The World Has Definitely Changed started as the 1986 version of the 10-year forecast report that A. Gary Shilling & Company, Inc., prepares annually for our clients. Spelling out its basic hypothesis -- for the first time since the 1930s, the world faces excess supplies of almost everything -- and the implications or themes that flow from it took so much space that the result was essentially a book in report format. Consequently, when client requests for extra copies soon exhausted our supply, we altered it slightly and reissued it in book form. We also published it as a book because we believed that the world had definitely changed in significant enough and permanent enough ways to warrant a book.

This book has similar origins. It commenced as our 1987 annual 10-year forecast report completed at the end of last year. Several client orders for substantial numbers of copies of it in book form nudged us toward another book. And, as with our previous book, we hope that the developments and implications this one discusses are important enough and lasting enough to deserve the attention that often only a book can command.

One final note. After The World Has Definitely Changed was written, I learned that most nonfiction books are not read past the first chapter. As a result, the obvious advice to authors is, summarize it in the first chapter or forget it! Quite by accident, our book was not summarized in the first chapter, but in the table of contents. Many readers -- and even a few reviewers -- have told us that they liked this approach and that it encouraged them to read specific chapters or even the whole book. We're trying to stick with a winning horse, so this book, too, is summarized in its table of contents -- but briefly enough, I hope, to pique your interest to read on.

A. Gary Shilling
February 1988

Acknowledgments

The book originated in the 1987 annual 10-year forecast report of A. Gary Shilling & Company, Inc., and I am extremely grateful for the underlying research and analysis that my colleagues provided for that report. Roger H. Fulton and Gilbert F. Benz contributed immensely, and Joseph Lin and Kathryn Poulos lent great aid.

I am also deeply indebted to Kenneth G. Oehlkers for the skill and care with which he assembled major sectors of our 10-year forecast report from earlier reports and for editing and overseeing the design and text of this book. Campbell O. Wilson was of great help, not only in crystallizing the title, but also in preparing the summary of reports on which much of it is based, and editing the many drafts.

Patricia K. Luvin provided her usual polite but effective guidance in making all of us stick to our tight deadlines. Karen G. Mishler helped in constantly reminding me that priorities must be set in order to complete a project of this size on time. I also thank Anne B. Spies, our industry analyst, who pitched in when needed to smooth the process under our tight schedule. Finally, Mary P. Johnson deserves my very special thanks for applying her masterful editing and production skills to this book and bringing it to fruition.

A.G.S.

After the Crash: Recession or Depression?

Introduction

PART I

MAJOR ECONOMIC FORCES
AFFECTING THE NEXT DECADE

Five new basic forces will have profound effects in the next decade and beyond. All point to excess global supply of almost everything for the first time since the 1930s.

1) Major sources of worldwide demand are exhausted.

The strong demand and shortages that dominated the world from World War II through the 1970s are over. Nothing on the horizon will replace, for example, rebuilding Europe and Japan in the 1950s and 1960s or inflation

---

* This book is a sequel to A. Gary Shilling's The World Has Definitely Changed: New Economic Forces and Their Implications for the Next Decade, and takes into account the October 1987 stock market crash and other events affecting the longer-term economic and financial outlook that have occurred since that book was completed in the fall of 1986. This introduction briefly summarizes that earlier work, and may serve as a refresher for those who have read it. For those who have not, we encourage them to read The World Has Definitely Changed in its entirety. Obviously, this 16-page summary can hardly do justice to the entire book.

in the 1970s. Inflation was generated by excessive U.S. government spending on the Vietnam War and Great Society programs, but then itself became a major source of demand as it spurred shortage scares and inventory building in anticipation of price increases.

So far in the 1980s the U.S. has been the world's only significant source of economic demand, pulling other countries into business recovery by increasing its foreign trade deficit from $36 billion in 1980 to more than $170 billion in 1987. But concern over the huge trade deficit, increasing protectionism, and reviving U.S. industrial competitiveness make it unlikely that the U.S. will continue this role of global economic locomotive, and no other sources of worldwide demand are in sight.

2) Meanwhile, global supply is surging.

At the same time that major sources of global demand have been exhausted, worldwide supply of almost everything has surged not only in Europe and Japan, but in the newly industrialized countries (NICs) such as South Korea, Taiwan, Hong Kong, Singapore, Brazil, and Mexico as well. The NICs are pursuing export-led development strategies and moving up the technological ladder, from textiles to steel and shipbuilding and now to consumer electronics and even autos. At the same time, their governments strictly limit imports and, in any case, their populations are too poor or too savings-oriented to offer significant markets to other countries' exports. In addition, the list of NICs is expanding to include Thailand, Malaysia, and Indonesia, with China not far behind.

3) Debt: Creating it fueled demand, but now servicing it increases supply.

Debt growth has been an important stimulus to demand throughout the postwar era, first rekindling expansion in the industrialized nations and then spreading it to developing countries, especially in the 1970s, when soaring prices and volumes of those countries' commodity exports convinced international lenders to provide them with almost unlimited funds.

However, with the collapse in prices of many internationally traded commodities in the early 1980s, the Third World countries that relied on commodity exports and borrowed funds went broke and were forced to end their import binges.

Indeed, these countries were forced to switch almost overnight from being importers and consumers to trying to become producers and exporters in order to earn the foreign exchange needed to service their debts -- a double negative.

The U.S. is not far behind the Third World in the debt cycle. The expansion of the last five years has been floated on a sea of debt issued by the federal government to finance its huge ongoing deficits, the corporate sector to pay off stockholders in leveraged buyouts, and consumers to finance their shopping spree. But all of these borrowing binges are about over: the role of debt is likely to shift from financing demand to encouraging supply as the nation increases production and reduces spending in order to service its huge debt load.

4) <u>Voter dissatisfaction means less government involvement in the economy.</u>

With no new sources of global demand, huge increases in supply, and the reversal in the role of debt from financing demand to encouraging supply, the world desperately needs new sources of demand. If it doesn't develop from natural forces, can't governments be expected to fill the gap? Not likely, since voters in every major country now distrust governments and want less government involvement in their lives, slower growth in government spending, and smaller deficits, if not surpluses.

5) <u>Demographic shifts are creating an older, more conservative population.</u>

The U.S. population continues to grow older as birth rates remain at low levels and the postwar baby boomers mature. And, as the postwar babies age and move into their peak earning years, they will become more conservative.

PART II

RESULTING THEMES FOR THE NEXT DECADE

The shift from a world of strong demand and shortages to one of excess supply has 21 basic implications or themes for the next decade.

1) <u>Despite the dollar's decline, U.S. industry will continue to face intense international competition.</u>

Three factors point to this conclusion. First, in a world of excess supply, all countries want to export. The only alternative is politically and economically unacceptable unemployment at home. Second, the U.S. is the obvious export target, being the world's biggest consumer. Third, America is still the globe's highest-cost producer in some industries. It has been for decades, though it didn't matter when strong demand and shortages dominated, and even high-cost producers could sell with ease. When shortages turned to surpluses, however, high-cost producers were no longer viable.

These three factors are a lethal combination. Strong-currency European countries and Japan are doing everything to avoid raising their prices in dollar terms and thereby risking the U.S. market shares they built so painstakingly over the years. They are cutting costs and profit margins and moving production to the much lower-cost NICs, which tend to link their currencies to the dollar.

2) <u>Deregulation of American industry will continue.</u>

Deregulation, which started with the brokerage industry in 1975 and then airlines and trucking in the late 1970s, continues with buses, railroads, telecommunications, financial services, and oil and gas. It is encouraged by voters' desire to see less government involvement, but also by basic economic necessity.

Regulation has always been imposed with the idea of protecting the customers of an industry, but invariably ends up protecting producers in the industry by holding a price umbrella over their costs. Costs in many regulated industries reached such extremes that something had to give, especially as the economic atmosphere shifted in recent years from excess demand to excess supply in the U.S. as well as internationally. Now, many deregulated industries are feeling the bracing winds of competition for the first time ever, and are making immense changes to adapt to it.

3) Cost control has become the new corporate creed.

Meaningful cost control on a widespread basis was absent in the U.S. from the 1930s until recently. It was unnecessary and hardly even considered in an era of strong demand, widespread shortages, and high inflation. Although concern over costs may have been absent, substantial cost increases were not. Labor compensation, the biggest cost item, has been the clear winner since the 1930s: labor's share of national income has risen from 65% to 75%, while profits' share fell from 15% to a low of 6% in 1982.

The switch from the world of excess demand to that of excess supply forced American business to turn its attention to the need for cost control, as intense competition in international markets and deregulation at home decimated inefficient producers. The demise of serious inflation and the resulting inability of most firms to pass on higher costs through price increases emerged as additional strong stimuli for cost control.

Labor costs are being attacked with a particular ferocity, since they comprise three quarters of total costs for American business as a whole. In addition, overhead costs are being slashed, transportation efficiency improved, inventory costs reduced, and factories and offices automated. As a result, many, although not all, U.S. industries are regaining international competitiveness.

4) The favorable climate for many of America's basic industries is over.

Many American industries still behave like cartels. In the past, industries such as autos, rubber, and steel had little foreign competition and were dominated by a handful of large companies that in effect exercised cartel-like control over their markets and set prices, design standards, etc.

Today, however, those cartel powers have been destroyed by global competition and domestic deregulation, and Detroit can no longer dictate to U.S. car buyers how long the tail fins will be. Cost control in the U.S. is having an impact on these industries, but many are still a long way from getting rid of cartel-like thinking and cost structures so that they can compete effectively with Europe and Japan. To make things worse, the locus of production in many of those industries is shifting from Europe and Japan to the NICs, where costs are much lower.

5) <u>But basic U.S. manufacturing will not disappear entirely.</u>

Many workers in basic industries are vastly overpaid by international standards, but eliminating their jobs and shifting them to other areas would chop off a big chunk of Americans' spending potential, since people in other industries are paid considerably less. Furthermore, importing all the basic manufactured goods we consume would add to the already-tremendous trade deficit, unless offsetting exports could be found.

The complete loss of basic industry production and jobs to imports probably could not be made up by high-tech exports or foreign tourism, at least not within the next decade. In addition, U.S. manufacturing management and labor aren't going to sit by while their businesses and jobs disappear; the growing protectionist sentiment in Congress is testimony to their concern and influence in Washington. Furthermore, national security interests probably dictate that basic industries of some minimal size be preserved.

6) <u>Productivity and corporate profits will improve significantly.</u>

Productivity growth has been disappointing since the early 1970s. However, the revival of the work ethic in the

1980s, the maturation of the postwar babies, the end of severe inflation, and, most of all, the continuing zeal for cost control on the part of American business imply that a return to trend or even above-trend productivity growth can be expected in the next decade.

This plus wage restraint will lead to 9%-to-10% annual growth in corporate operating earnings in the next decade, assuming no major economic or financial disruptions. And, for the first time in 50 years, profits' share of the total economic pie should rise and labor's share should fall. There will be vast differences in specific industries and companies, depending not only on volume growth, but also on their ability to control costs and increase productivity in an atmosphere where raising prices will continue to be very difficult.

7) Unemployment will remain high despite slow growth in the labor force.

Contrary to popular belief, slower entry of younger people and older women into the labor force is not likely to result in tight labor markets in the next decade. The postwar rebuilding and catch-up demand that dominated earlier decades is obviously long over, and the global excess supply conditions we see continuing will limit real GNP growth to about 3.0% per year by keeping the pressure on our foreign trade sector. Combined with the expected annual rise in output per manhour of 2.5%, this implies an increasing, not decreasing, unemployment rate.

Inadequately educated and trained workers will further aggravate unemployment problems over the next decade. Low-skilled manufacturing jobs are disappearing to the NICs, and U.S. job growth in the future will focus on the extremes of high-skilled technical and professional occupations in such industries as electronics and computer software on the one hand, and low-skilled jobs in such areas as security services, hotels, and building maintenance on the other. There will probably be plenty of people available for low-skilled jobs, but some high-skilled jobs may go begging for lack of adequately trained applicants.

8) Purchasing power of middle-income households will fall as higher-income households gain.

The American dream is over. Up until now, each successive generation of Americans has been brought up thinking that it could live higher on the hog than its parents and retire rich. In the next decade, however, many of those who hope to surpass -- or at least equal -- their parents' living standards will be disappointed.

Cost control by American business is the driving force behind this persistent weakness in real incomes. Many middle-income people will continue to see their purchasing power decline, or not grow as rapidly as they expected, because of two factors. The first is further reductions in real incomes in existing jobs; the other, continuing movement in employment opportunities from high-paying positions that are disappearing due to ongoing foreign and domestic competition to low-paying jobs. But at the same time, they will continue to see executives, professionals, and other high-income people gaining in purchasing power.

It's bad enough for the losers to see the American dream turn into a nightmare, but there would have been at least some consolation if everyone were in the same boat. It will only add insult to injury for the losers to realize that they not only must live lower on the hog but also that the real incomes of those on the top are rising. Social and political unrest could well result.

9) Serious inflation is over.

High rates of inflation are unlikely to return for many years to come as a result of a continuing world of surpluses, global cost control, and universal voter pressure to reduce government's share of the economic pie -- a reliable indication of inflation in the past. Over the next decade, we look for annual inflation rates to average about 2%, and that forecast may prove to be on the high side.

10) Commodity prices, including oil prices, may continue to plummet, and deflation is a threat.

The world of surpluses that we expect to endure through the next decade will continue to depress commodity prices. This is especially true since so many commodity producers are financially weak, less-developed countries (LDCs), whose reaction to declining prices is to produce and export even more in order to earn the same amount of foreign exchange to service their huge foreign debts. This turns into a vicious circle because the increased supply drives prices lower, requiring even more production, which adds further to excess supply and drives prices down even lower, etc.

Oil is just another commodity, albeit the most widely watched one. Its price is well above equilibrium only because of the OPEC cartel. But OPEC looks increasingly shaky as its financially weak members cheat by exceeding their export quotas. A collapse in oil prices, perhaps to single-digit levels, is likely.

Deflation can already be seen in other tangible assets, including farmland, Houston office buildings, gold, and investment-grade diamonds. Declines in commodity and other tangible asset prices of a size that seems quite likely in the future could affect prices of goods and wages, and from there spread to services.

Deflation can be very disruptive to pay expectations and buying behavior. The prospect of lower prices encourages buyers to hold off purchases. This can generate a downward cycle, with weak demand leading to lower prices, leading to weak demand, etc.

11) Real interest rates will fall significantly.

We believe that serious inflation is over, but neither the Federal Reserve nor bond investors agree. Otherwise, real interest rates, the difference between interest and inflation rates, would not be so much above historical levels.

Bond investors were burned by negative real returns not once, but twice, in the 1970s, and they want to be thoroughly convinced that inflation is dead before they give up the real interest rate premiums they currently enjoy. Further collapse in oil prices could help build the conviction that inflation is over, since the rise in oil prices in the 1970s came to symbolize the serious inflation problem. So could meaningful control of federal spending and the budget deficit.

A recession in coming quarters could also go a long way toward convincing many that inflation is over. It would close off the first expansion since the late 1950s that did not deteriorate into inflation, and thereby surprise many who believe that business upswings always end with an inflationary burst.

12) The postwar boom for commercial and apartment construction is over, but single-family housing will remain strong.

Four basic forces drove construction in the postwar era, but all four have now been largely reversed. Inflation, especially in the late 1960s and 1970s, made real estate very attractive as the classic hedge against accelerating prices and living costs, but now serious inflation appears to be over. Favorable tax policy, topped off by the 1981 provisions, has aided real estate for decades, but the 1986 Tax Reform Act killed many of the tax advantages of real estate. Generous lenders have facilitated the highly leveraged financing of real estate in the postwar era, but badly burned lenders and regulators have begun to take a much more cautious approach. Demographics, especially the postwar baby boom, have driven construction for decades. Now, however, all that is left is a few more years of single-family construction, as the last of the baby boomers buy their first houses.

13) Investment Strategy Switch -- Financial assets are in, tangible assets are out.

The place to be in the inflationary 1970s was in tangible assets such as coins, antiques, and real estate -- the classic hedges against inflation -- and on a highly leveraged basis. Stocks and bonds were big losers in that inflationary climate. Treasury bond yields, which had been rising steadily since the early 1950s, skyrocketed in the 1970s when inflation surged, so bondholders saw the prices of their assets collapse even before adjustment for inflation, and lost again, since the higher yields didn't even offset inflation rates. The S&P 500 stock index, adjusted for inflation, fell over 50% between the mid-1960s and 1982. The rise in interest rates made fixed-income instruments very attractive relative to stocks, and inflation bled corporate profitability and transferred it to government and labor.

In the early 1980s, however, the winning investment strategy reversed dramatically with the sudden collapse in inflation and the declining prices for farmland, oil, and many other tangible assets. Tangibles became the losers, while financial assets have been the winners. Bonds have been fabulous investments, and should continue to be, as yields on long-term Treasury bonds fall to 4% to 5%. Stocks will benefit from this decline in interest rates and from the expected 9%-to-10% compound growth in operating earnings -- assuming no major economic or financial disruptions.

14) The emphasis on free markets will continue to grow.

The U.S. and other Western industrialized nations can no longer afford widespread interference with free markets, nor will their voters accept it. In the U.S., changes that suggest a fundamental shift to a free-market orientation include:

A) Deregulation of a growing number of industries;
B) Reduction of securities market regulation;
C) Decline in antitrust enforcement;
D) Weakening of the political power of industries with cartel-like behavior;
E) Weakening of the political clout of labor unions;
F) A shift in agricultural policy from price to income support in order to be more price-competitive internationally;
G) A tax reform act that reverses a 50-year trend toward using tax policy to achieve social and economic goals, and instead relies on market forces;

H) Increasing incentives for people to be economically self-sufficient; and

I) The Administration's policy of letting major corporations go into bankruptcy rather than bail them out, as was done earlier.

15) Deflation Manifestation I -- Protectionism is a major threat.

A major threat to the world economy is growing protectionism here and abroad -- a key manifestation of global excess supply and deflationary trends and an expected one: it was last seen in the excess supply years of the 1920s and 1930s. Furthermore, as more and more people see their jobs lost to imports, their wages cut, and their workloads increased to improve competitiveness, or as they see themselves forced to take low-paying, undesirable, dead-end service jobs, pressure from individuals for protectionism will add to the problem.

Two alternatives to all-out protectionism are being widely discussed:

A. Achieve significant growth abroad, especially in Europe and Japan. Yet Germany fears higher inflation, and it will be difficult for Japan to wean its economy from its "export-or-die" mentality.

B. Improve U.S. competitiveness by shrinking the gap between our wages and those of our competitors. However, this doesn't provide a solution to the basic lack of world demand. Second, increases in U.S. productivity and cuts in wages and the dollar's value could make us competitive with Europe and Japan, but production in many basic industries is shifting rapidly from those areas to the much lower-cost NICs like South Korea and Taiwan.

Protectionism slows global trade and economic activity as it leads to offsetting retaliation by trading partners. And, to the extent that it works, protectionism reduces U.S. demand for the world's goods and leads to a slowdown abroad that then reflects back on this country.

In an excess supply world, protectionism may be unavoidable, so controlled protectionism, aimed at countries with big exports to the U.S. but few American imports that can be cut off, may be a lesser evil than all-out protectionism. On the other hand, special trade advantages may be necessary for Latin American countries and others that have borrowed heavily from major nations to help them at least try to service their huge foreign debts.

16) Deflation Manifestation II -- Financial problems will continue and could lead to crisis.

In the 1970s, when tangible asset prices were soaring and real interest rates were negative, many individuals, corporations, and whole countries bet the farm, the ranch, or, in Mexico's case, the hacienda, on those conditions lasting indefinitely. Mexico expected oil prices to reach $100 a barrel and therefore anticipated no problem in repaying the tremendous amounts of money it had borrowed in international markets.

But the climate has swung from the best of all possible worlds for that speculation to the worst, leaving the "inflation-forever" believers high and dry. Real borrowing rates have gone from negative to punishingly high levels while many tangible asset prices have shifted from non-stop climb to frightening collapse. The problem has become one of marking down the prices of tangible assets -- and the loans that financed them -- in step with the dramatic decline in inflationary expectations.

So far, the Federal Reserve has been very skillful and very lucky in isolating financial crises and handling them one at a time. The risk, however, is that the problems come so thick and fast that the Fed and other credit authorities are inundated, people start to ask, "Who's next?" and confidence in the financial structure evaporates.

17) Fiscal stimulus will remain off limits worldwide, and monetary policies will continue to be impotent.

What the world needs most is strong growth, but it's unlikely to be provided by substantial tax cuts or government spending increases in major countries because voters in North America, Europe, and Japan want less government involvement in their economies and smaller, not bigger, budget deficits.

This leaves it up to monetary policies to provide the needed stimuli. But central bankers who learned the hard way how devastating inflation can be are still fighting the last war -- inflation. They are still far too little concerned with the next war -- inadequate demand and deflation. Furthermore, as in earlier periods of low inflation or deflation, individuals and businesses in most major countries are holding more and more money relative to economic activity -- the reverse of their practice in the earlier postwar period. Slow to recognize this shift, central banks will hardly provide skimpy amounts of credit, much less pump out enough to stimulate global economic demand.

18) The triple transcession will continue.

"Transcession" is the term we coined several years ago to describe a transition that causes slow economic growth and/or more frequent recessions. We are now in a triple transcession -- from shortages and high inflation to surpluses and low inflation or deflation; from the dominance of basic and regulated industries and construction to that of high-tech and services; and from rising to falling purchasing power of middle-income families.

These three transcessions, we think, will dominate the U.S. economy for a number of years, if not the entire next decade, and in many ways resemble a Kondratieff Wave depression.

19) Depression is more likely than many may think.

The parallels between the world now and that of the late 1920s are indeed frightening, and the possibilities that a

1930s-style depression would occur cannot be completely ruled out. All the safeguards introduced in the 1930s to protect the stock market have been circumvented, perhaps paving the way for another Crash. (See Chapter 10, "The Next Recession Will Test Whether the World's Financial Structure Can Avoid a Depression," for further details.)

20) Share Shifts -- Capital spending, profits, and saving gain, while government and many consumers lose.

The basic forces and the resulting themes discussed above will produce some major shifts in the shares of various real GNP components in the next decade. We assume no major economic or financial disruptions, however.

Consumer spending's share of economic activity will decline as cost control holds personal income growth down. Furthermore, the aging of the postwar babies, and more important, the cost-control induced squeeze on middle incomes while upper incomes grow will concentrate income in the hands of the higher-income big savers. As a result, consumer spending will grow more slowly than incomes.

As noted, housing should enjoy at least a few more good years, but other construction will suffer from the end of the favorable real estate climate and, for the next five years or so, from the excess capacity in hotels, shopping centers, and office buildings. Capital equipment spending, however, is likely to be the fastest-growing major sector of the economy, driven by the zeal for cost control and productivity and fueled by strong growth in corporate profits and consumer saving.

The foreign trade deficit should shrink as many American companies regain international competitiveness, but will still be substantial 10 years hence, as Europe and Japan also cut costs and as production continues to shift to the low-cost NICs. Voter pressure is expected to shrink government's piece of the economic pie somewhat over the next decade.

21) Winners and Losers

In the environment we foresee for the next decade, the winners include upscale consumers and the related higher-priced travel and recreation, specialty merchandise, and financial services. Cost-saving equipment and services will benefit, as will the highly trained people needed in those areas. Goods and services related to single-family housing should show strength for at least the next five years. Interest rate declines in coming years will aid utilities, insurance, regional banks, and S&Ls. Tourism from foreign visitors may be an important growth area. Barring severe protectionism or financial crises, stocks and bonds should be winners in the next decade.

The losers list includes tangible asset sectors such as U.S. agriculture, commercial and multifamily real estate, and producers of commodities, including energy, here and abroad. Money center banks and overleveraged companies, basic industries with cartel-like mentality, and their labor unions may all be in trouble. Poorly trained people will no longer find high-paying jobs available, and many middle-income people's purchasing power will be severely squeezed by cost-cutting measures.

1

The U.S. Has Lost Control
of its Financial Markets
to Foreigners, and
Run Out of Easy Policy Fixes

The key financial event of 1987 was not the stock market crash. Rather, it was the growing realization that the U.S. had lost control of its financial markets to foreigners, and that the nation had run out of easy policy options to do anything about it.

These factors, in one way or another, probably caused the October stock market crash. At minimum, they appear to be the only significant new considerations at work when the speculative stock market suddenly collapsed with none of the usual signs of a peak. Normally, conviction that the market will rise forever becomes so widespread at peaks that all of the skeptics -- we became one in January 1987 -- are thoroughly discredited. Furthermore, overconfidence and the bidding up of the prices of quality stocks normally lead to a shift in emphasis toward lower-quality issues and finally to the junk before a bull market ends. In addition, speculative stock markets that are about to break have historically sucked in small uninformed investors. When a small man casts a long shadow, the sun is about to set!

This time, these signs of bull stock market senility were absent, but investors were clearly aware of and were getting nervous over America's financial position vis-a-vis the rest of the world. Over a year ago, the U.S. became a net debtor nation for the first time since World War I, and in the third quarter of 1987, for the first time in 70 years, we paid foreigners more in interest and dividends on their assets in the U.S. than Americans received from their foreign holdings. Investors realize that as the huge foreign trade deficits continue -- at a $171 billion rate in 1987 -- both the net debtor position and the net outflow of interest and dividend payments will rise. We are now a poorer nation because, in contrast to the past when net inflows of interest and dividends raised our living standards, a growing part of what we now produce must be used for foreign debt service.

Dependent on Foreign Financing

Investors also fretted over whether foreigners would continue to invest in this country and in particular to finance our continuing large federal budget deficits. In reality, they have to invest in the U.S. since they must do something with the dollars they ended up with in 1987 as a result of our trade deficit. They're not going to store $171 billion in paper currency.

But, foreigners can create immense problems as they decide the exchange rates at which they're willing to invest in U.S. assets, and which assets they're willing to buy. They could wreak havoc on U.S. Treasury markets if they suddenly decided that they no longer wanted to buy newly issued Treasury bonds, and instead put their dollars only into Los Angeles office buildings. Investors, then, were well aware that the U.S. financial tune is no longer being called in New York, but in Tokyo, London, and Frankfurt.

The Dollar -- All Out of Options

Early in 1987, the Administration sensed the loss of control of U.S. financial markets to foreigners, and decided to attack the problem through competitive devaluation. A weaker dollar, they reasoned, would improve our trade position by making American products cheaper abroad -- thereby encouraging exports -- and by increasing import prices, thereby reducing their appeal. They also thought that talking down the dollar would put pressure on Germany and Japan to stimulate their economies and stave off more severe protectionist actions by Congress. A policy of talking down the dollar is nothing short of competitive devaluation, a term just as applicable to the

Administration's recent actions as it was to those taken by many countries in the 1930s. By itself, of course, it is a form of protectionism.

The pressure on Europe and Japan to create more demand showed good instincts by the Administration, led by U.S. Treasury Secretary James Baker. As we pointed out in our 1986 book, The World Has Definitely Changed, we are in a world of long-term surplus of almost everything, and new sources of demand are desperately needed. The U.S. has been almost the sole major source of global demand increases in the last five years, but has financed that new demand with huge increases in debt and transmitted it abroad through the surge in our trade deficit. With the U.S. exhausted by debt, other sources of demand are sorely needed. Unfortunately, Germany can't see past its borders and has no intention of creating significant domestic, much less global, demand for fear of creating inflation, and Japan acted to stimulate its economy modestly only after being bludgeoned by Washington's threats of protectionism.

Increases in American exports have been slow in coming, however, and imports continue unabated. The Administration failed to realize that foreign producers have no interest in getting out their silver platters and handing over to American competitors the market positions they have painstakingly built over the years in this country and abroad, with or without the weak dollar. The policy makers also failed to understand the speed with which production in the steel, auto, and other basic industries is shifting out of the strong-currency countries in Europe and Japan to the much lower-cost newly industrialized countries (NICs) like South Korea and Taiwan, which tend to link their currencies to the dollar.

In effect, the Administration had hoped for a "free lunch" of improving trade performance through competitive devaluation. But like the British in their similar and ill-fated attempt after World War II, the Administration fails to comprehend that the rest of the world will not stand still while this process is going on. In a world in which virtually every nation has surpluses of men and machines that can only be used by exporting, the only effective approach to solving the U.S. trade problem is high and continuing productivity growth in American industry.

Knocking down the dollar, then, did not prove to be an effective option for solving the loss of domestic control over U.S. financial markets. Quite the opposite; starting about March 1987, investors began to worry whether foreigners would continue financing the federal budget deficit as the value of their Treasury bond holdings declined in terms of their own currencies. The result of this, and fears of imported inflation, was a rise in the 30-year Treasury bond yield from 7.5% to 10.5% that threatened to induce a U.S. recession. This, of course, further limited the use of competitive devaluation as a policy tool.

True, since the Crash U.S. dollar and bond market prices, which in 1987 had moved down in lock step, became uncoupled as the dollar continued to fall while bonds rallied. However, this uncoupling may not continue indefinitely any more than it did earlier. From February 1985 to April 1986, the dollar fell while bond prices rose, and from then until March 1987, the dollar continued to slide while bond prices were about flat. In March 1987, however, the coupling of the two finally took hold with a vengeance.

Monetary Policy -- Little Leeway

The Federal Reserve also has few options for dealing with the U.S.'s loss of control of its financial markets. On September 4, 1987, the Fed, under its new chairman, Alan Greenspan, decided to give the market a whiff of anti-inflationary grapeshot and to support the dollar with a half-point increase in the discount rate. The results were unexpected and devastating. Investors seemed to react by saying, "My God, now even the Fed is nervous over the loss of domestic control of financial markets." Short-term interest rates and bond yields shot up, and the stock market, which had reached a peak in the previous week, started its slide, culminating with the October 19 Crash.

After the Crash, the Fed had even less room to tighten since it feared a recession in the 1988 election year. But suppose the Federal Reserve reverses the field and decides, especially if a 1988 recession develops, that the way to deal with it and with our international debts and the servicing of them is to inflate our economy, thereby deflating the values of those debts? This, too, is unlikely to be a viable policy option because of likely offsetting actions by investors who vividly remember the devastating inflation of the 1970s and fear its return.

The 1970s saw the first major peacetime inflation in the nation's history. Previously, inflation was a wartime-related phenomenon. It started with the outbreak of fighting and stopped when peace was declared and demobilization took place, or after an inflationary blowoff initiated by the removal of wartime controls on prices and wages. As a result, investors in the 1970s were caught unaware and suffered negative real, or inflation-adjusted, interest rates as inflation rates exceeded bond yields, as shown in FIGURE 1. Since then, nervous lenders and bond holders have demanded very high real interest rates to protect themselves from any resurgence of inflation.

<h2 align="center">FIGURE 1</h2>

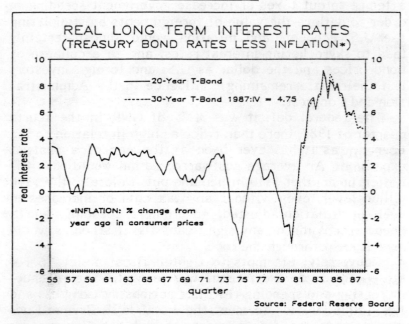

In this state of mind, investors demand even higher real interest rates whenever inflation begins to appear on the distant horizon, as it did the spring of 1987 when the dollar decline threatened to drive up the prices of imported and then domestic goods. Similarly, any attempts by the Fed to reflate the economy and deflate the value of foreign debts by easing credit would probably lead to a surge in real interest rates that would negate the stimulative effects of that easy credit policy.

As we pointed out in Is Inflation Ending? Are You Ready?, the ultimate result would be the odd combination of widespread fears of serious inflation and the resulting high real interest rates, but in fact a stagnant economy with virtually no inflation. With memories of the frightening inflation of the 1970s still vivid, even deliberate attempts to recreate it would probably be fruitless.

Fiscal Policy -- The String Is Out

Fiscal policy has even more clearly run out of options to deal with the loss of control of financial markets. Any attempt to cut taxes or increase government spending in order to deflate the value of foreign debts by stimulating the U.S. economy and inflation would almost certainly lead to skyrocketing interest rates, and to a collapse of bond prices and the dollar as U.S. and foreign investors lost their little remaining confidence in the Administration and Congress.

The federal deficit was 3.5% of GNP in the fourth quarter of 1987, more than twice as high in relation to the economy as it has ever been at the end of a postwar expansion. An average postwar recession would push the deficit up another $110 billion and put it close to the $300 billion level, even without any tax cuts or increases in real, or inflation-adjusted, government spending, and a deeper recession or any significant fiscal stimulus would send it right through the roof.

Conversely, attempts to tighten fiscal policy to restore confidence are fraught with danger. The revenue-increasing and spending-restraint actions by Congress and the Administration to meet the fiscal 1988 Gramm-Rudman targets for deficit reduction did little to restore confidence among investors, businessmen, and consumers, so the net effect will be to depress business activity, not encourage it. In the world of surpluses we see continuing, and in the face of a possible dramatic decline in consumer spending, the last thing that is needed in an immediate sense is government spending cuts and higher taxes. Just as the President's initial statement of confidence after the October 1987 collapse in stocks echoed Herbert Hoover's reassurances after the 1929 Crash, tax increases now might parallel those of the early 1930s, which only deepened the Depression.

It seems, then, that the nervousness among bond and stock market investors this year parallels the growing realization that control of American financial markets has passed to foreign hands and that there is little that can be done through manipulation of the dollar, or monetary or fiscal policy actions to reduce that loss of control quickly.

In fact, the last straw in this realization came the weekend before the October 19 Crash. Treasury Secretary Baker apparently became so frustrated with the lack of fiscal stimulus by the Germans that he blasted them publicly. Normally, it wouldn't seem like such a good idea to openly criticize the bankers from whom you have borrowed a bundle, but that's exactly what he did. It clearly showed the impotence and frustration of Washington policymakers, and might have been the impetus for the Crash as some foreigners pulled out of the stock market, and Americans followed in an attempt to beat the remaining investors, both domestic and foreign, to the exit.

Regaining Control Is Possible

Despite the lack of easy policy fixes, regaining control of U.S. financial markets is possible in the long run. The cost control and restructuring now being pursued by American business with increasing zeal will do wonders to make it again internationally competitive in a number of industries.

In addition, to a great degree the U.S. is shifting from becoming a nation of spenders to a country of savers. (See Chapter 5.) Increased domestic saving will reduce the need for borrowing abroad and will help finance the tremendous growth in capital spending we see in the next decade, as part of the cost control and corporate restructuring effort. Furthermore, higher saving rates mean slower consumer spending growth; this will not only help reduce the trade deficit, but also help the U.S. to regain control of its financial markets. However, with global surpluses expected to continue, the rest of the world can hardly be expected to cooperate with our efforts to improve our trade balance.

Finally, the federal government can reduce the need for foreign financing by reducing the deficit. Every voter wants this, but not at his expense, so big spending cuts and tax increases seem unlikely. At best, Congress and the Administration will hold down the growth in spending as revenues rise with longer-run economic growth, thereby gradually whittling down the deficit.

Of course, a significant defense spending reduction stemming from a major accord with the U.S.S.R. could produce a dramatic deficit reduction in the years ahead. Secretary Gorbachev seems very interested in reaching such an accord so he can transfer resources from the military to the civilian economy as he attempts to build and modernize his country, which is now essentially an underdeveloped one outside the military sector. President Reagan would love a major arms accord as a capstone for his career, otherwise tainted at the end by the Iran-Contra affair and the stock market crash. Maybe they'll both achieve their goals and jointly win the Nobel Peace Prize to boot!

2

Serious Inflation Is Over,
and Deflation Remains
the Threat

From the middle of 1984 to the end of 1987, the U.S. economy grew at a 3% annual rate as measured by real GNP, but starting about the middle of 1986, the driving forces changed. Earlier, consumer spending, services -- especially financial services -- defense outlays, and residential and nonresidential construction were the leaders, while manufacturing languished under intense international competition, and agriculture, mining, and the energy sector were in nosedives.

More recently, consumer spending growth has faltered, although it continues to rise at an unsustainable rate, given the weakness in income growth. (See Chapter 5.) In 1987, real, or inflation-adjusted, consumer outlays rose 1.8%, while real after-tax income gained only 1.2%. Furthermore, construction faltered as high mortgage rates and consumer caution hurt single-family housing. And excess capacity and the 1986 Tax Reform Act killed multifamily housing and commercial construction of hotels, shopping centers, and office buildings in many areas of the country. Service sector growth in general is easing, and financial services are slipping rapidly as a result of the stock market crash, the winding down of the leveraged buyout business, a peaking in the property and casualty insurance cycle, and the pressure on banks to cut costs due to Third World country loan losses and other problems. Furthermore, federal budgetary pressures are squeezing defense spending.

At the same time, however, the agriculture, mining, and energy sectors have bottomed out, at least temporarily. Most important, the source of economic growth has shifted to the foreign trade sector. A combination of the weak dollar and zealous cost control and restructuring by American business finally brought the slide in the foreign trade deficit to a halt in 1986:III. As shown in FIGURE 2, the growth in imports, after adjustment for inflation, has slowed on balance since then, while exports have climbed. Geographically, the manufacturing-oriented American heartland has turned around, while the white-hot East and West Coast economies are cooling along with consumer spending, the construction, financial and other services, and defense industries on which they depend so heavily. The next recession may temporarily disrupt these sector and geographic shifts, but assuming that it does not turn into a financial and economic disaster, many of them should remain in place for a number of years.

FIGURE 2

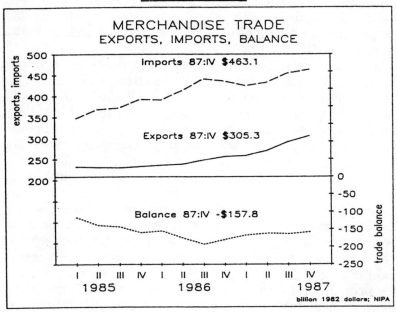

The cuts in obsolete capacity and other restructuring moves needed to gain international competitiveness, however, have been largely responsible for the capacity strains in some basic American industries such as paper, chemicals, and textiles. This plus commodity price increases (see FIGURE 3) have led to renewed fears of inflation. Nevertheless, these concerns may relate more to a short-term phenomenon coming at the end of the business cycle and not reflect a long-term problem. In the long run, there are a number of factors that will hold down price growth and may even lead to deflation:

F I G U R E   3

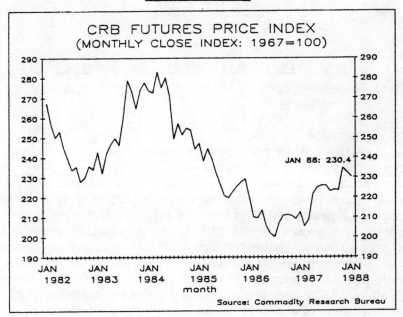

CRB FUTURES PRICE INDEX
(MONTHLY CLOSE INDEX: 1967=100)

JAN 88: 230.4

Source: Commodity Research Bureau

New major sources of global demand are lacking. Despite the sector shift in economic driving forces in the U.S., the American economic expansion is about out of gas since the consumer, who accounted for two thirds of economic activity, is nearing the end of an unsustainable borrowing and spending binge. Japan shows little interest in taking over from the U.S. the role of stimulating world growth, and Europe has even less interest. The Third World countries would spend money if they had it or could borrow it, but they're broke and can't find any ready lenders.

- Industrial capacity continues to mushroom in the newly industrialized countries (NICs), compensating for strained plants in the U.S. FIGURE 4 shows that six of them accounted for 4% of world exports in 1970, but 8.7% in 1986. Moreover, their exports are becoming more sophisticated, having moved from textiles to shipbuilding and steel and now to consumer electronics and even autos. Furthermore, the list of NICs is growing to include countries like Thailand, Malaysia, and Indonesia. China isn't far behind.

FIGURE 4

PERCENT OF WORLD EXPORTS

	Korea	Sing-apore	Hong Kong	Taiwan	Brazil	Mexico	Total
1970	0.3%	0.5%	0.9%	0.8%	1.0%	0.5%	4.0%
1975	0.6	0.7	1.0	0.9	1.1	0.4	4.7
1980	0.9	1.0	1.1	1.1	1.1	0.8	6.0
1986	1.8	1.1	1.8	2.0	1.2	0.8	8.7

- The U.S.'s shift back toward basic industries and away from construction and services is a shift from low- to high-productivity sectors. The shift in economic growth away from nonmanufacturing to manufacturing is a shift from low productivity growth to high productivity growth sectors, as shown in FIGURE 5. As a result, much more output growth can be handled without straining capacity. Manufacturing, which accounts for 25% of nonfarm private output, had productivity growth of 3.9% per year from 1980 to 1987 compared with the long-term trend of 2.8%, as cost control and restructuring emerged as dominant corporate activities. Even in the 1984:III to 1986:II period, when manufacturing output grew only modestly, manufacturing output per manhour rose 4.3% per annum. This shows the tremendous power of cost control, since productivity growth is normally very subdued at low rates of output growth when overhead costs cannot be spread over many more units of output.

In contrast, nonmanufacturing productivity only grew at a pitiful 0.4% annual rate in the 1980-87 period, and actually fell in five of the last seven quarters. In contrast to the intense foreign and domestic competition and weak demand growth that manufacturing has faced in much of

FIGURE 5

	Nonfarm Business	Mfg.	Nonmfg.
1970-80	1.0%	2.3%	0.4%
1981	0.7	2.2	0.1
1982	-0.2	2.2	-1.2
1983	3.2	5.7	2.3
1984	2.1	5.5	0.8
1985	1.2	5.1	-0.2
1986	1.6	3.7	0.9
1987	0.9	3.3	0.0
1980-87	1.3	3.9	0.4
1986:I	6.6%	4.9%	7.3%
II	0.3	2.8	-0.5
III	-0.8	2.3	-1.8
IV	-0.2	1.9	-0.9
1987:I	0.4	3.3	-0.6
II	1.4	6.5	-0.3
III	4.2	3.3	4.4
IV	0.2	0.2	0.1

this decade, many nonmanufacturing businesses have enjoyed booming demand and limited competition. Consequently, their interest in productivity improvement has been weak. The recent moderation in nonmanufacturing growth, however, may focus attention on the need for productivity growth. This is certainly true in financial services, where cost cutting has begun with a vengeance. Furthermore, manufacturers themselves are heavy users of services of all sorts and are starting to press those vendors as they press all of their suppliers for better quality and lower prices.

Productivity growth in nonmanufacturing, then, seems likely to revive in the years ahead. Furthermore, any sustained speed-up in manufacturing output growth should accelerate productivity in those goods-producing industries, as overhead costs are spread over more units of output. A repeat of the 5%-plus productivity growth seen in manufacturing in 1983 and 1984 doesn't seem unreasonable, and this would mean that output could expand 5% per year without any net increase in hours worked. This, of course, merely extends the phenomenon of recent years.

From 1980 through 1987, manufacturing output grew by 27.2%, but in that same period, manufacturing employment actually declined 5.7%, from 20.6 million to 19.5 million.

• <u>Heavy use of part-timers -- especially those who are working part-time involuntarily -- also holds down costs and inflation.</u> FIGURE 6 shows the tremendous growth since the early 1970s in involuntary part-time employment (people who want full-time work, but don't have it because employers don't need them full-time). Between 1973 and 1986, involuntary part-timers rose from 2.3 million to 5.3 million. Some, but not all, part-timers work for temporary employment firms and other personnel supply services listed on the last line of FIGURE 6. As shown there, this category has exploded from 245,000 in 1973 to over 1 million in 1986, as cost cutters rely more and more on outsiders to do jobs more cheaply and more efficiently. The habit of using outside people and their growing availability reduces the urge to hire people ahead of actual need, which characterized and magnified labor shortages in the past. Furthermore, part-time workers are less costly because they receive fewer fringe benefits and are employed only during the time of the day or season of the year when actually needed.

FIGURE 6

TRENDS IN PART-TIME WORK, 1973-86
NONFARM INDUSTRIES

	Thousands of Workers		
	1973	1979	1986
TOTAL Employment	81,574	95,477	106,434
Full-time Employment	64,065	74,097	81,974
Part-time Employment	12,724	15,779	18,847
Voluntary	10,381	12,406	13,502
Involuntary	2,343	3,373	5,345
With Job but not at Work	4,805	5,601	5,613
Employment: Personnel Supply Services	245	527	1017

SOURCE: U.S. Department of Labor

• <u>Labor strains are unlikely.</u> Clearly, several ongoing developments will easily prevent any meaningful strains on the labor supply in the longer run: the shift of economic growth to underutilized manufacturing industries whose already-rapid productivity growth will be enhanced by faster output growth; the likely improvement in nonmanufacturing productivity; and a more complete utilization of part-time workers. The forthcoming years may more closely resemble our long-term outlook, shown in FIGURE 7, than the 1970s and 1980s to date, when overall productivity growth was miserable.

F I G U R E   7

KEY ECONOMIC ASSUMPTIONS FOR THE NEXT DECADE
(Percent Average Annual Change)

	Actual 1973-87	Projected 1987-97
Real GNP	2.4%	3.0%
Output/Manhour	0.8	2.5
Compensation/Manhour	7.1	3.0
Real Compensation/Manhour	0.2	1.3
General Price Level	6.4	1.7
Labor Force	2.1	1.3
Average Annual Hours	-0.4	-0.5
Unemployment Rate (period end)	6.2	9.9

SOURCES: U.S. Dept. of Commerce; U.S. Bureau of Labor Statistics; A. Gary Shilling & Company, Inc.

As shown, we expect 3.0% real GNP growth for the 1987-97 period, about in line with the past several years and weaker than earlier postwar decades, as will be discussed in Chapters 4 and 8. Output per manhour should grow at a 2.5% annual rate, slightly above the long-term trend of 2.3%, but very reasonable, given continuing zeal for cost control and the maturation of the postwar babies and other demographic factors. Combining real GNP and productivity growth gives a forecast for the growth in manhour demand of 0.5% per year. This is actually less than the likely increase in the supply of manhours.

With fewer older women and fewer younger people entering the labor force, its growth should run 1.3% per year, and the average work week will probably continue to shrink. Consequently, available manhours are likely to rise 0.8% per year, and lead to a rise in the unemployment rate to an average of 9.9% by the middle of the next decade. With faster productivity growth, then, a slowdown in labor force growth is needed to prevent serious unemployment problems. Contrary to what many believe, generalized strains on the labor force are unlikely, but as observed in The World Has Definitely Changed, the lack of adequately trained and educated people will cause bottlenecks in the years ahead.

Wage restraint continues, union strength wanes, and paternalism is over. Not only are labor shortages unlikely in the quarters and years ahead, but wages will also probably continue to be restrained. FIGURE 8 reveals the dramatic slowdown in wage increases in private industry from the decade's start, when they were close to double digits, to the current 3% annual rate. In fact, the squeeze on wage increases has been so great that real wages actually fell in the first three quarters of 1987. Even as inflation cools, the squeeze on incomes should continue, with ongoing cost-cutting zeal. Intense global competition has altered the attitudes of the vast majority of American businessmen who have a "take-no-prisoners" attitude toward costs and no longer believe that they have a patriotic duty to keep their employees at least abreast of inflation. This change in attitude has even reached such previously paternalistic companies as AT&T, Kodak, and Caterpillar. Instead, they are determined to make a reasonable profit regardless of the circumstances, and to cut costs, improve productivity, move operations to lower-cost areas, or even close them if necessary to achieve their objective.

FIGURE 8

WAGE INCREASES AND INFLATION
PRIVATE INDUSTRY WORKERS
(% Changes)

	Wages (Dec.-Dec.)	CPI Dec.-Dec.)	Real Wages (Dec.-Dec.)
1980	9.0%	12.4%	-3.0%
1981	8.8	8.9	-0.1
1982	6.3	3.9	2.3
1983	5.0	3.8	1.2
1984	4.1	4.0	0.1
1985	4.1	3.8	0.3
1986	3.1	1.1	2.0
1987	3.3	4.4	-1.1

	Annual % Change (qtr. end- qtr. end)	CPI (qtr. end- qtr. end)	Real Wages (qtr. end- qtr. end)
1986:I	3.9%	-1.7%	5.7
II	2.5	2.4	0.1
III	3.8	2.8	1.0
IV	2.2	1.1	1.1
1987:I	4.1	5.9	-1.7
II	2.8	5.1	-2.2
III	4.0	5.2	-1.1
IV	2.4	1.5	0.9

Most employees accept this change, and are more interested in job security than in pay hikes, having seen many of their colleagues disappear from the workplace, white- as well as blue-collar. The rapid decline in the unionized portion of the workforce, shown in FIGURE 9, has enhanced this change in attitude. Old, obstreperous unions in basic industries like steel and autos that enjoyed high pay for low-skilled jobs in the days when those industries exercised cartel-like control over prices have become dominated by foreign competition. Deregulation has had the same effect on industries like airlines and trucking, as the bracing winds of competition have swept through them. At the same time, the industries that have been experiencing rapid growth in recent years are those in the high-tech and service areas that don't have the cartel power or the massive concentration of blue-collar jobs that fosters strong unions.

FIGURE   9

UNION MEMBERSHIP
AS A % OF NONFARM EMPLOYMENT

| | Thousands | | |
	Union Membership	Nonfarm Employment	Percent
1955	16,802	55,722	30.2%
1960	17,049	60,318	28.3
1965	17,299	66,727	25.9
1970	19,381	75,215	25.8
1975	19,979	82,438	24.2
1980	19,972	95,938	20.8
1985	16,996	103,971	16.3
1986	16,975	106,434	15.9

	Union Membership Non-Gov't Employees	Private Nonfarm Employment	Percent
1985	11,226	87,921	12.8%
1986	11,087	90,060	12.3

SOURCE: Bureau of Labor Statistics

Note: 1985 & 1986 derived by different method than earlier data.

As shown in FIGURE 9, the percentage of nonfarm employees who belong to unions fell from 30% in 1955 to 16% in 1986. And, the percentage is much lower if government employee unions, which have existed only since the mid-1960s, are deleted. A mere 12% of private nonfarm employees now belong to unions. The decline in union membership can be expected to continue. Although we see some revival of rust-belt manufacturing, U.S. labor leaders have had little success in unionizing newly opened plants, whether foreign- or U.S.-owned.

Commodity price increases, to a certain extent, are just offsetting the weak dollar. FIGURE 10 shows what's been happening to commodity prices in yen and D-mark terms since their dollar peaks were reached in 1987, and also the declines in commodities in strong-currency terms since their 1987 peaks. Gold has fallen 8% in yen terms

FIGURE 10

COMMODITY PRICES IN $, YEN, AND DEUTSCHEMARKS

	Peak	% Change from 1987 Peak to 2/12/88			% Change from 10/30/87 to 2/12/88		
		$	Yen	D-Mark	$	Yen	D-Mark
CRB Index	11/27/87	-2%	-4%	1%	4%	-1%	3%
Gold	12/18/87	-11%	-8%	-7%	-5%	-10%	-6%
Platinum	8/3/87	-30%	-39%	-36%	-12%	-16%	-12%
Silver	4/17/87	-43%	-48%	-46%	-8%	-13%	-9%
Oil	8/3/87	-26%	-36%	-32%	-16%	-20%	-17%

between its dollar peak on the day of the Crash, October 19, 1987, and February 12, 1988, and 7% in terms of D-marks. Oil is down 36% in yen and 32% in D-marks since its peak in dollar terms in August, 1987.

• The uncoupling of bond prices and the dollar suggests fundamental concerns with slow economic growth and perhaps even deflation, not a return to inflation. From January 1987 through mid-October, bond prices declined in lockstep with the weakness in the dollar, as shown in FIGURE 11. As noted in Chapter 1, investors worried over whether foreigners, especially the Japanese, would continue to finance the federal budget deficit in view of the ongoing decline in the value of their holdings in yen terms. Furthermore, bond investors saw a return to serious inflation in this country as import prices were raised by foreign producers to offset the decline in the dollar, and as American competitors followed those price increases with delays of no more than 30 seconds. Between December 1986 and mid-October 1987, the dollar declined 8.8% on a trade-weighted basis, while yields on 30-year Treasury bonds rose from 7.5% to 10.5%.

Between the October stock market crash and the end of January 1988, however, prices on 30-year Treasury bonds rose sharply while the dollar declined another 6.0%. This divergence may not continue indefinitely, as noted in Chapter 1, but it suggests, for now at least, that concerns have reversed completely, that fears of inflation have been replaced by fears of deflation. The Crash brought home to many the real possibility of a recession or even a 1930s-style depression in the months ahead. In the world of sur-

FIGURE 11

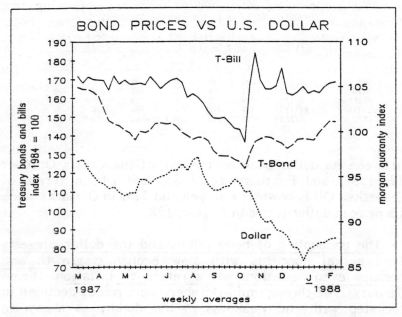

pluses of just about everything, the danger is deflation, and not inflation.

- The weaker dollar has failed to produce proportionately higher inflation in the U.S. Since the dollar started down in the first quarter of 1985, it has declined 35% on a trade-weighted basis through the fourth quarter of 1987, but import prices have increased only 5.6%. As will be discussed in Chapter 3, strong-currency countries continue to cut costs and profit margins and to move production to the much lower-cost NICs in order to avoid raising the prices in dollar terms and risking the loss of their U.S. market shares.

The Administration's talking-down-the-dollar policy is ultimately deflationary. Although it may be aimed at improving our trade balance, putting pressure on Germany and Japan to expand their economies, and staving off even more protectionist measures in Congress, it nevertheless amounts to competitive devaluation and is protectionist, as noted in Chapter 1. In the final analysis, protectionism is deflationary, not inflationary.

To begin with, what we gain in an improving trade balance through competitive devaluation or other protectionist moves is what the rest of the world loses. But the U.S. has been the globe's only economic locomotive in the last five years, and the means by which we provided stimulus to the rest of the world was our deteriorating trade balance. The surge in U.S. imports and weakness in American exports increased demand for the rest of the world's products and pulled foreign countries into recovery. Any improvement in the U.S. trade picture will come at the expense of other countries since in a world of surpluses other sources of demand growth are lacking.

With Canada and the NICs virtually pegging their currencies to the U.S. dollar and the OPEC countries' major export, oil, priced in dollars, this leaves OECD-Europe and Japan to absorb increased U.S. exports and reduced imports resulting from a weak dollar. Any meaningful reduction in the U.S. trade deficit that follows could easily throw Japan, and especially Europe, into a recession. And, it isn't even a zero-sum game, but a net negative. With any such slowdown in worldwide economic activity -- and with it, demand for the Third World commodity exports -- some of the losers would be financially weak countries such as those in Latin America, which could easily be thrown into financial crises that could precipitate global deflation.

Furthermore, competitive devaluation may give way to other forms of protectionism. If the weak dollar approach fails and Congress, in an election year, moves on to other forms of protectionism, it might decide to block imports of, say, consumer electronics products and autos. In turn, the exporters' governments could return the favor in our major export areas -- computers, aircraft, and agricultural products. As retaliation grew and global exports slowed, so would worldwide economic activity, and a universal recession could quickly develop.

Finally, successful U.S. protectionism would lead to a decline in U.S. living standards. Now, we are trading IOUs, not goods and services, for high-quality, low-cost imports. If tariff walls were to go up, we would have to reduce our consumption to our production level, or work a lot harder to produce our current level of consumption. Either way, we would be paying more for lower-quality goods, in many cases. The United Auto Workers might make out like bandits, but many American auto buyers would be facing higher prices for cars that many of them consider inferior to imports. This may sound inflationary, but it's ultimately the reverse. Lower U.S. living standards could well touch off an American recession, and certainly would reduce imports and foreign economic activity.

3

The U.S. Trade Deficit
Won't Go Away

Only after a 25% decline in the dollar on a trade-weighted basis, from February 1985 to September 1986, did U.S. exports begin to increase. Moreover, this was the result not only of the weak dollar, but also the ongoing efforts to control costs. Meanwhile, imports continue at high levels. In 1982 dollars on a National Income and Products Accounts basis, the merchandise deficit has only declined from $193 billion at its peak in 1986:III to $158 billion in 1987:IV as was shown in Figure 2. Why this lack of meaningful response to the weak dollar?

• <u>We're in a world of excess supply in which many countries have no option to exporting except politically and economically unacceptable high levels of unemployment at home.</u> Furthermore, the U.S. is the obvious export market, since this country represents 30% of world consumer demand. In addition, many U.S. industries remain high-cost producers.

• <u>Strong-currency countries have responded to the weak dollar by cutting costs, reducing profit margins, and moving component production -- and even complete goods production -- to the NICs rather than raise prices in dollar terms and risk losing the U.S. market.</u> These NICs link their currencies to the dollar; even if they didn't, it wouldn't make much difference since their costs are so much lower than those in the U.S. In manufacturing, American labor costs are 10 times those of Korea and seven times those of Taiwan. It's hard to imagine the decline in the dollar against those currencies that would be needed to close the gaps. It would push the cost of a hotel room in Seoul to over $1000 per night! Along with Canada, which also links its currency to the U.S. dollar, the newly industrialized countries represent 33% of U.S. foreign trade.

• A vicious equilibrium has developed: at just about the rate the dollar has declined against European currencies and the yen, production is moving out of Europe and Japan to the much lower-cost NICs. This is an equilibrium, because the NICs gain production at just about the same rate as the dollar falls, and it is vicious because even though the U.S. currency is declining, America is not the primary beneficiary. The strong-currency countries are losing, but it's the NICs that are the winners. The net effect is that the 35% decline in the dollar on a trade-weighted basis since February 1985 has only resulted in a 5.6% rise in import prices, as noted in Chapter 2.

• American business has responded to the devalued dollar by raising prices, not market shares. When prices of imports have risen, American competitors in the auto, steel, and many other industries have matched those increases with little delay, thereby opting for higher profits rather than higher shares of U.S. markets. Conversely, in foreign markets, many American exporters have increased their dollar prices to maintain their prices in strong-currency terms, rather than hold down those prices in bids to increase U.S. exports. These actions may be understandable, in view of the earlier depressed state of many U.S. firms' earnings, the pressure on American corporations for short-term earnings performance, and the risk that holding down their prices against strong-currency competitors would not really help in the long run, as production shifts to the low-cost NICs anyway. Nevertheless, it weakens greatly the improvement in the U.S. trade balance that might result from the weak dollar.

• A number of products that Americans consider near necessities are simply not made in this country. No VCRs or compact disk players are made here, and very few color television sets are manufactured domestically.

One effect of the weak dollar is to encourage foreign producers to set up operations in the U.S. Initially this was spearheaded by the Japanese as a way of getting around protectionism. It's unlikely that Congress would close down U.S. auto plants employing Americans even if they are owned by the Japanese. More recently, however, the weak dollar has encouraged this phenomenon and it has spread beyond autos and television to a number of other industries. It does act to cut down on U.S. imports and also encourages exports because foreign producers -- the Japanese and Europeans -- are much more export-oriented than many of their U.S. counterparts. At the same time, however, the effects are limited since many of the parts assembled in foreign-owned U.S. plants are still imported. Furthermore, the high value-added engineering and design work is still done abroad, and profits are remitted to foreigners.

It still can be argued that a weak enough dollar will redress the U.S. trade balance regardless of the implications for the rest of the world, but finding that equilibrium is almost impossible. The purchasing power parity concept used by economists for determining equilibrium is difficult to calculate. The idea is that if the U.S., for example, is inflating 2% faster than its trading partners, then the dollar should decline against their currencies by 2% per year to keep purchasing power parity. The proper values of currencies are established by looking at the relative inflation rates from a starting point, which must be assumed to be one of equilibrium. Ah, there's the rub! The last time we had anything that resembled equilibrium was probably in the early 1960s, and that's so long ago that structural changes make it irrelevant.

Furthermore, the vicious equilibrium described above suggests that the dollar could continue to decline against the European currencies and the Japanese yen indefinitely, and we would still not reach equilibrium on a global basis because production is shifting out of those strong-currency countries to the low-cost NICs at just about the same rate as the dollar is falling.

In addition, the U.S. dollar's use in import and export transactions is only a tiny fraction of the total global use of the dollar. Some estimates are that only 5% of dollar transactions fall into this category. Part of the rest is everybody else's trade. If the Germans and the Japanese are trading between themselves, they're probably doing it in dollars. Also, the dollar is the international currency, and the tremendous number of capital transactions swamp all the trade flows involving the dollar. As a result, it is the proverbial tail wagging the dog, in that an equilibrium value for the dollar in terms of U.S. trade may be completely superseded by the dollar's use in other areas.

Is the dollar near its bottom? Having said this and realizing that the universal conviction now is that the dollar must go much lower to redress our trade imbalance, two points can be made that suggest that the dollar may be near its bottom.

First, when everyone's convinced markets will fall forever, they're usually about at a turning point. All of those who could sell have done so, and there only remain potential buyers. The G-7 major industrialized countries may not prove to be accurate forecasters, but their renewed decision to support the dollar is probably based on their conviction that the dollar is oversold. The governments involved realize their intervention in currency markets can't buck fundamental trends, and they certainly don't want to attempt support if the dollar has a lot further to fall, and risk being immediately discredited and embarrassed.

Secondly, if a global recession of unknown depth is in the offing in the next year, as we believe and will discuss in Chapter 6, then there very well could be a run for the dollar as a safe haven. We've seen repeatedly in the last several years that in times of trouble, people head for the safest currency in the world, the dollar, and for the U.S. markets, which are the deepest, broadest and safest available. For example, normally when two countries are in military conflict, international money flees from both their currencies. But the day after the U.S. raided Libya in early 1986, money flowed into the dollar as a safe haven. The same was true when the U.S. started to escort tankers through the Persian Gulf in 1987. Again, the dollar was strong in a time of trouble. More recently, even though the stock market crash started in the U.S. and then spread abroad, the dollar was strong for the next several days, again as a safe haven in a very uncertain world.

A significant climb in the dollar against the currencies of America's trading partners would add one more reason to the long list that suggests only a slow improvement in the U.S. trade deficit. We may prove to be too cautious, but our forecast is for a 1997 deficit that is still almost half the 1987 level.

4

High-Tech Industries and Services Will Replace Basic Industries and Construction as the Foundations of American Business Growth

In the first 15 or 20 years after World War II, American basic industries had everything going for them. Foreign competition was minimal since the war had largely destroyed their counterparts in Europe and Japan, and what little capacity there was abroad was fully utilized in rebuilding those economies. The NICs had barely begun to industrialize during those years, much less export. Furthermore, American basic industries participated in the rebuilding of Europe and Japan through substantial exports. Finally, those industries experienced strong demand at home as private spending caught up from the low spending Depression years of the 1930s and from World War II, when military needs preempted consumption.

The Losers

By about the mid-1960s, however, Europe and Japan were rebuilt and started to become formidable competitors for U.S. basic industry. Also by then, domestic catch-up demand had been satisfied. This began to put pressure on those industries that has intensified in the past 10 years, with the rise of the NICs as major exporters of an increasingly sophisticated array of goods.

As production in basic industries like steel and autos continues to move from Europe and Japan to newly industrialized countries like South Korea, Taiwan, Brazil, and even Mexico, it seems likely that American output in these areas will continue to decline. Cost control and productivity improvements would have to be monumental to compete with countries that now have the same or better basic industry technology than U.S. producers, but pay production workers $1 to $2 per hour -- less than one tenth the pay of their U.S. counterparts. Furthermore, it is in these basic U.S. industries that the cartel-like mentality and resistance to change remain the strongest.

Residential and nonresidential construction have also been mainstays of the U.S. economy in the postwar era, but are rapidly losing their pillars of support:

The tax code is no longer favorable to real estate. Tax laws have been favorable to real estate for decades, but those introduced in 1981 encouraged construction of multifamily housing units, office buildings, hotels, and shopping centers to the point of creating huge excess supplies that will take years to absorb. And, with the Tax Reform Act of 1986, the bulk of these favorable tax laws has been removed.

High inflation, a strong propellant of rising real estate prices in the 1970s, seems unlikely to recur.

Lenders are becoming more particular and charge more. Savings and loans, commercial banks, and other real estate lenders were extremely generous in earlier years, and asked few questions on even the shakiest real estate deals. Furthermore, the regulation of thrift institutions kept mortgage rates low. Now, however, many lenders have been badly burned by real estate defaults, and many more disasters are in the wings. As a result, the new-found caution seen among many of these lenders can only intensify. Furthermore, the end of regulation of thrift institutions and the securitization of the mortgage markets have raised real estate lending rates by tying them much closer to market rates.

Many of the baby boomers are now housed. Demographics, especially regarding postwar baby boomers, have created strong demand for schools, housing, shopping centers, office buildings, etc. in the last four decades. The presence of the postwar babies will continue to be felt in the housing market as a number of them move into their first homes, but the bulk of them will be housed early in the next decade. Beyond that, housing will be dominated by demand for second and retirement homes, although the growth in those areas is determined more by income than by age levels.

Furthermore, virtually all of the postwar babies have entered the labor force, so their influence on office space is over. Also, they were followed by very low birthrate groups, whose smaller numbers will tend to depress demand in many real estate areas. Finally, cost control efforts may temper demand for new office buildings and other structures, as businesses conclude that they can get by with cheaper space and with less space per employee.

The postwar babies have not yet had their final stimulating effects on construction, however. In about four decades, funeral home construction will be booming!

The Winners

On the growth side of the ledger, high-tech industries such as electronics, computers, bioengineering, fiber optics, superconductivity, and telecommunications are likely to become dominant before the next decade is over. These are industries in which the U.S. will probably continue to have the commanding lead in research and development. At the same time, the products of many of these industries will be used extensively by other American businesses as they pursue higher productivity.

Many of these industries are not new, but have not yet grown large enough to collectively become a major source of overall economic growth. Capital equipment spending on high-tech equipment is still only about 50% of the total.

The service sectors of the economy have been growing faster than goods-producing industries for a long time, and are approaching a size that will make them another dominant driving force in the U.S. economy.

Services are also relatively immune from international competition. In fact, the U.S. may expand its exports of financial and other services, as well as travel services geared toward foreign visitors. Also, consumption of services tends to grow faster than that of goods as incomes rise. At higher purchasing power levels, people may not add more cars to their driveways, but will probably spend much more on travel, recreation, and other services. In addition, accounting, legal, consulting, and other business services should continue to expand with the growing sophistication of American business.

There is no question that the sources of American growth -- and indeed, growth in other major countries -- are shifting, but it's far from clear that the transition will be a smooth one, with high-tech industries and services picking up as basic industries and construction recede. A gap between the two could hold back overall economic growth for a number of years, as will be discussed in Chapter 8.

5

Income Polarization Will Continue, While Overextended Middle-Income Americans Continue Unsustainable Borrowing and Spending

Cost control and restructuring, American business's response to global competition, is squeezing the incomes of many middle-income Americans, and pushing them to lower-cost status. The auto worker who was twisting on bolts in Detroit at $25-$30 an hour including fringes, or $50,000-$60,000 a year, has seen his job depart to the Orient or to a non-union auto plant owned by the Japanese. If he's lucky and resourceful, he's been retrained as a computer programmer, but he's only starting at about half his former rate, $25,000-$30,000 a year; otherwise, he may be behind the counter at McDonald's making little more than the minimum wage of $3.35 an hour. Few have accepted this squeeze on incomes gracefully, because most of us as Americans believe that our birthright includes living higher on the hog than our parents and retiring rich.

In the 1970s hordes of older women marched into the labor force to try to continue the growth in their families' purchasing power. That didn't work. Then they worked longer and harder by having fewer children and having them later in life, but that didn't work, either. Now families are borrowing to finance lifestyles they can't afford but don't want to give up. With the change in the tax law, borrowing has shifted from credit cards, auto loans, and other forms of installment debt to second mortgages and home equity loans, but it still continues. In 1987, real consumer spending grew 1.8%, less than half the 4.2% advance in 1986. But, the need to borrow actually increased because the gap between spending and income widened as real after-tax income growth fell from 4.0% in 1986 to 1.2% in 1987.

After the inflation in home prices in the 1970s, Americans still have enough unencumbered equity in their houses to continue heavy second mortgage borrowing for several years. However, by liquidating the remaining equity in their houses, Americans won't have it to pass on to their children. Unless there is another round of serious inflation, which we doubt, those children will not be able to afford to buy the houses they grew up in, or to have the home equity to tap for many expenses, including their children's educations.

Middle-Income Families Are Squeezed . . .

As shown in FIGURE 12, in 1973, 53% of American households had incomes in the $20,000-$60,000 range in 1985 dollars and, as FIGURE 13 shows, received 57% of total personal income. In 1985, only 49% fit the middle-income category, and their share of total personal income had fallen to 52%. Furthermore, we expect this shift to continue and to accelerate. In 1995 middle-income households are forecast to slide to 38% of the total number and to account for only 36% of income. Many of these families are sliding to a lower-income status and account for the fact that the number of those with incomes under $20,000 grew from 39% of the total in 1973 to 42% in 1985 and is forecast to rise to 50% in 1995.

FIGURE 12

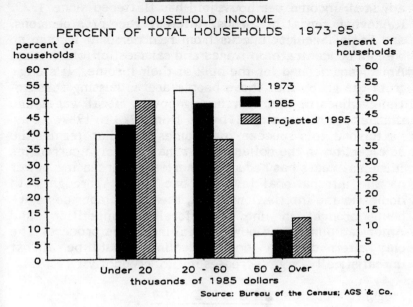

HOUSEHOLD INCOME
PERCENT OF TOTAL HOUSEHOLDS 1973-95

percent of households

percent of households

1973
1985
Projected 1995

Under 20   20 - 60   60 & Over
thousands of 1985 dollars

Source: Bureau of the Census; AGS & Co.

FIGURE 13

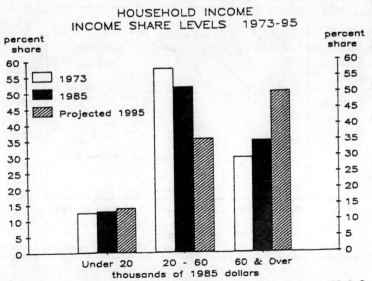

HOUSEHOLD INCOME
INCOME SHARE LEVELS 1973-95

percent share

percent share

1973
1985
Projected 1995

Under 20   20 - 60   60 & Over
thousands of 1985 dollars

Source: Bureau of the Census; AGS & Co.

FIGURE 14 shows that overall real, or inflation-adjusted, income per household has flattened since 1973. Removing rents, dividends, interest receipts, pensions, and Social Security checks from real personal income so we can concentrate on wages and salaries, on which most Americans depend for the bulk of their incomes, it's clear from the graph that those people are witnessing substantial declines in their purchasing power. Real wages and salaries per household fell by 5% from 1973 to 1987.

Beyond this squeeze in incomes in dollar terms, the 33% decline in the dollar against major foreign currencies in recent years has reduced Americans' purchasing power on the international level by one third. Through both domestic and international cuts, then, U.S. labor costs are being brought in line with foreign competition, and American purchasing power is falling in the process. The only alternative to income declines would be almost unrealistically large increases in U.S. productivity.

F I G U R E   1 4

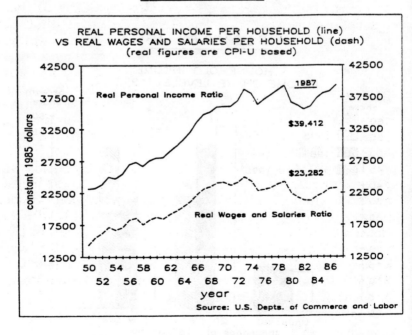

Because borrowing has been used to maintain spending,

the squeeze on middle-income purchasing power -- one of the most profound developments in the last 15 years -- has gone largely unnoticed, except by those lending the money. But, excessive borrowing can't continue forever, and sooner or later many families must face the end of the American dream.

When they do, their reactions may be extreme. It's bad enough as they see themselves and other middle-income families sinking into the swamp in a leaky barge, but it will add insult to injury when they look up to see all those higher-income people sailing into the sunset on a beautiful new party yacht.

. . . While Upper-Income Households Gain

At the same time that many middle-income people are being pushed down, those at the top will continue to grow in number and incomes. The postwar babies are aging and moving on to their peak career earnings. More important- ly, high-paid jobs are expanding rapidly for welltrained and educated managers and professionals. Many of those people are in high-tech and other industries that can compete effectively in the international arena, while a number are helping other industries become more com- petitive. In 1985 dollars, the average income for house- holds with pretax incomes over $60,000 rose from $124,000 in 1973 to $131,000 in 1985, and we estimate that it is likely to reach $149,000 in 1995. Their share of total income will rise from 30% in 1973 to 50% in 1995 -- an amazing jump in only two decades!

The shift in income to higher-income households will greatly increase saving and the funds available for invest- ment. In this country, there is clearly a division of labor between savers and spenders, as shown in FIGURE 15. Households with $75,000 or more in pretax income in 1985 saved 38% of their after-tax dollars -- 48% if they were headed by someone over 65 -- but those with less than $10,000 in pretax income had a negative 97% saving rate, or spent $1.97 for every after-tax dollar!

FIGURE 15

HOUSEHOLD SAVING RATES
(By Age and Income, 1985)

	All Incomes	Under $10,000	$10,000-20,000	$20,000-30,000	$30,000-40,000	$40,000-50,000	$50,000-60,000	$60,000-75,000	$75,000 & Over
All ages	5%	-97%	-21%	-5%	5%	9%	12%	16%	38%
Under 25	-7	-88	-11	4	12	16	20	25	46
25-34	3	-104	-14	-2	6	10	13	17	38
35-44	5	-153	-20	-9	-1	4	8	12	34
45-54	7	-193	-26	-12	-1	5	8	12	33
55-64	12	-108	-28	-8	7	14	18	22	43
65 & over	1	-56	-25	1	17	21	23	27	48

SOURCES: Bureau of Labor Statistics; A. Gary Shilling & Co.

Consequently, the income shift and, to a lesser extent, the aging of the American population should increase the percentage of take-home pay not spent on newly produced goods and services -- the saving rate -- from 5.1% in 1985 to 10.5% in 1995, a level that is rare in the postwar period. The saving rate has fallen further since 1985 and hit a post-Korean War low of 2.8% in 1987:III. If people return to the norms that yielded a 6%-to-8% average saving rate range in the earlier postwar era, the rate would exceed 10.5% in 1995. It would be higher still if the overspenders decided that the American dream is over for them and that they need to save even more than normal to repay the huge debts they have accumulated.

Incomes and Assets Shift in the Same Direction

Augmenting this income shift is the shift in net worth that is going on at the same time. The 1970s, with all of that decade's inflation, were very beneficial to the prices of tangible assets such as coins, antiques, and real estate. And, tangible assets are widely held -- two thirds of American families own their own houses -- so middle- and lower-income families benefited.

The 1970s was a lousy decade for stocks, bonds, and other financial assets, as interest rates rose and inflation transferred earnings to labor and government. With the dramatic decline in inflation rates in the 1980s, however, the action has reversed, and the winners are -- despite the stock market crash -- financial assets, while tangibles languish. Financial assets, however, are very narrowly held. Only one household in five owns stocks, bonds, or mutual funds, and those tend to be people with high incomes as well. For all but the top 10% of Americans in terms of net worth, their houses are worth 22 times their stock holdings. Consequently, the shift in the value of asset holdings toward financial assets and away from tangibles is reinforcing the growing relative strength of high-income households.

...aggregate funds, and then I want to be people with high incomes as well. For all but the top 10% of Americans, the value of net worth, both human are worth 2 1/2 times their stock holdings. Consequently, the risk that a whole or asset holdings to yield dramatic assets and income from equities lessens to raise the growth relative strength of higher income households.

6

The Stock Market Crash Increased the Odds of a 1988 Recession

The collapse in the stock market in October 1987 has increased the likelihood that the U.S. economy will enter a recession before the end of 1988.

That may sound like a trivial statement since recessions are always preceded or at least accompanied by stock market declines. But, the reverse isn't always true. It's been pointed out that the stock market predicted nine of the last five recessions. I vividly remember the sharp stock market correction in 1962 when the Dow Jones Industrial Average fell 27% in six months. It was preceded by a hot market for new stock issues in 1961 that was so explosive that even though it was my first excursion into investments, I naively calculated that I would be rich enough to retire even before I completed graduate school.

Of course, I gave it all back in the 1962 stock market break, and like many others, then wondered when the recession would commence. It didn't, of course, because the economy was basically sound. But this time it isn't.

Financial and economic imbalances abound in the U.S. and abroad. Foreign trade imbalances among industrialized countries are extreme. Growing protectionism is a major threat to global trade and economic expansion. Third World debt problems are nearly hopeless. Japan appears to be on the brink of major financial problems and a possible economic depression. The U.S. has been the only major source of world demand growth in the last five years. It has financed that expansion in demand through unprecedented borrowing at very high interest rates: by the federal government to finance its ongoing deficits, by business principally to pay off stockholders with leveraged buyouts, and by consumers eager to maintain living standards they can no longer afford. The U.S. has transmitted this demand to the rest of the world by a skyrocketing trade deficit. Moreover, as discussed in Chapter 1, Washington has virtually run out of policy options to deal with any financial crises or economic decline the Crash may have foreshadowed, whether through dollar manipulation, monetary policy changes, or fiscal stimulation or contraction.

The $171 billion U.S. trade deficit in 1987 means that, on balance, $171 billion was bled away from American purchasing power. Dollars spent on imports are removed from the domestic economic stream and transferred to foreigners, and do not result in the domestic production, employment, or income creation needed to pay for those foreign goods. Consequently, the $171 billion must be either borrowed back from foreigners, adding further to the huge debt problems or, $171 billion of American assets must be sold to them. In a very real way, the U.S. is mortgaging its future and selling its family jewels to finance a wild party catered by foreigners.

More specific to initiating near-term recession, the cost-cutting-induced squeeze on middle-income purchasing power and the borrowing that the affected households are doing to finance lifestyles they can no longer afford but don't want to give up has created a great deal of vulnerability. In fact, starting about two years ago consumer borrowing and spending patterns became so unsustainable that it became a question of how and when people would be forced into agonizing reappraisals, not if they would be.

Four Potential Whistle Blowers

A number of different bodies could force that reappraisal. First, the Federal Reserve could tighten credit enough to squeeze out consumer borrowing. But a recession would probably also result, and that would be anathema to the Fed, especially in an election year, given the already oversized problems of Third World debtors and other financial crises that the credit authorities have to worry about. Second, banks and others who lend to consumers through credit cards, auto loans, home equity loans, etc., could curtail consumer credit. But even though delinquency rates are high and rising, consumer lending is still very profitable, and many lenders have few attractive alternatives, considering the financial problems with U.S. agriculture, real estate, and energy businesses, and with Third World countries.

Third, it is possible that consumers might blow the whistle on themselves. A husband could wake up one morning and say to his wife, "Dear, we've been borrowing and spending too much, and we simply must cut back." This seems unlikely since he would be admitting that the American dream of ever-increasing purchasing power was over for his family -- a powerful admission that even if he made it, other family members might rescind.

Almost by process of elimination, this leaves us with a fourth and most likely precipitator of consumer retrenchment -- an outside shock that would be sufficient to scare people into making agonizing reappraisals. Of course, given the time for consumer debt to mount to high enough levels, the Fed or lenders would cut off consumer borrowing or households might act themselves. In our view, however, it's more likely that an outside shock comes along before any of these three other whistle blowers.

By definition, shocks are impossible to forecast -- otherwise, of course, they wouldn't be shocking -- but we have felt for well over a year that the consumer was so far out on the borrowing and spending limb that a shock of sufficient magnitude to break that limb would occur before the end of 1988 with a three-to-one probability. Since consumption amounts to two thirds of GNP, any significant pullback by consumers would easily precipitate a recession. And, given the interdependence of the world's economies and the sluggish growth in Europe, any U.S. recession would probably spread globally very quickly.

The stock market crash last October 19 ought to be enough of a shock to scare consumers because it was so spectacular. The decline in the Dow Jones Industrial Average that day, 22.6%, was nearly twice the drop of 12.8% on the worst day in 1929, October 28. It dominated newspaper headlines and radio and TV news programs for weeks. Clearly, stockholders who lost a bundle were scared -- even more so those who subsequently lost their jobs in the Wall Street post-Crash cost-cutting binge -- but stockholders only constitute about 20% of American households. Perhaps more important was the scare to nonstockholders who were reminded of the 1929 Crash and the Great Depression that followed. Obviously, the 1929 Crash would only be an interesting piece of financial history if it hadn't served as the harbinger of the 1930s financial and economic disaster.

Crash Scares Nonstockholders

A nationwide survey of consumer buying intentions by The Los Angeles Times soon after the Crash revealed that 29% of stockholders planned to reduce purchases of major items, but 36% of nonstockholders decided to cut back. These results may sound strange at first but make perfect sense on further thought. Nonstockholders are more likely to have blue-collar jobs that will be cut in a business slump than the white-collar jobs typically held by stockholders. And, nonstockholders normally have fewer assets to fall back on if their jobs are lost. (But how about those ex-Wall Street yuppies?)

A consumer-led recession would be unique, at least in the postwar era. Normally, late in the expansion phase of the cycle, businessmen become so convinced that it will last forever that they splurge on plant and equipment and build inventories with gusto. This makes the Federal Reserve worry about an overheating economy, which leads to credit tightening, a rapid rise in short-term interest rates, and the onset of a recession, as housing and other interest-sensitive sectors collapse.

With this pattern in mind, many don't see any recession until 1989 since the Fed normally doesn't like to disrupt an election year -- but things aren't always normal. Ask Nixon about his loss in the Fed-induced 1960 recession, or Carter about his defeat in the midst of the 1980 recession that followed from massive credit tightening in the first quarter.

Fed Not Squeezing

Nevertheless, the Fed shows no signs of mounting a credit crunch in 1988. Chairman Greenspan's close ties to the White House and more important, the Fed's fear of what a recession would do to intensify already-drastic Third World debt and other financial problems suggests anything but a credit squeeze. But the imbalances are different this time -- not overconfident businessmen, but excessive debt expansion by the federal government, American business, and consumers; high interest costs applied to that debt; and a huge foreign trade deficit. The consumer looks like the most vulnerable of those imbalances, and if the Crash has scared him into a recession-inducing retrenchment, the Fed will be virtually powerless to prevent or even postpone it.

Any Way Out?

Of course, consumers may shrug off the Crash and continue on their merry borrowing and spending ways. But, that only postpones the eventual confrontation with reality, and only builds up more debt that will require even more retrenchment to pay off later. As noted in Chapter 5, the cost-control-induced squeeze on incomes is such that continuing growth in consumer spending requires higher debt to income ratios and lower saving rates.

Alternatively, Washington may try to ride to the rescue, especially in this 1988 election year. As discussed in Chapter 1, however, the Federal Reserve has limited room for easing credit significantly in anticipation of a recession, without raising fears that excessive ease will lead to inflation. As a result, the outcome could be higher, not lower, interest rates. Inflationary expectations will fade once a recession is clearly under way and give the Fed more running room, but probably not to the point that it could dump money out of airplanes without rekindling those fears. Furthermore, monetary ease normally doesn't affect economic activity for at least six months, and even more in a recession. Maybe astute policy could help prevent a recession from turning into something worse, but the Fed probably couldn't act soon enough to prevent one or even to postpone it.

Finally, as also noted in Chapter 1, this nation has lost control of its financial markets to foreigners, and the Fed has to deal with the possibility that aggressive monetary policy could raise further inflationary fears among foreigners who already fret over the ongoing federal budget deficits. They might then send the dollar lower, which would push interest rates higher as worries over whether foreigners would continue to finance the budget deficit accelerated, and as concerns over higher import prices grew.

Similarly, there is little that the Administration and Congress can do to prevent a recession or even mitigate it. The Federal deficit remains close to $200 billion. As noted in Chapter 1, on the basis of all the previous postwar recessions, a downturn of even average intensity would increase the deficit by another $110 billion, even if there were no tax cuts or increases in real government spending. Washington is already restrained from fiscal stimulus by current budget levels, and would be even more so by a deficit pressing $300 billion, even in a recessionary atmosphere. Quite the opposite: the Crash spurred the Administration and Congress to seriously consider reducing the deficit in order to restore confidence in securities markets. But since they did too little to improve anyone's confidence, the net result will be weaker, not stronger, business activity.

Finally, even substantial weakness in consumer spending could be offset by a big enough improvement in the foreign trade sector, stemming from the weak dollar and corporate cost control and restructuring. Since consumer spending is six times as large as exports, however, it would take a big reduction in the trade balance to offset any substantial weakness in consumer outlays. A 2% decline in consumption or $60 billion at current levels -- not at all unlikely if consumers are really shocked into realistic appraisals of their income and debt levels -- would require an offsetting 50% reduction in the trade deficit.

However, as noted in Chapter 2, in a world that lacks major alternative sources of demand, whatever the U.S. gains through a smaller trade deficit, the rest of the world loses, and foreign competitors are hardly likely to sit still for that magnitude of cuts in their production. Furthermore, a $60 billion reduction in our trade deficit, assuming that it comes entirely at the expense of the strong-currency countries in Europe and Japan, would bring them to the brink of recession, or maybe even push them over the edge.

On balance, then, the stock market crash enhanced the chances of a 1988 recession, but only by providing the likely shock to consumers that was going to come from some source sooner or later. More fundamentally, it is difficult, in view of the immense financial and economic imbalances in the world today, to believe that the Crash merely blew away the speculative fluff that accumulated in the preceding year just to leave the stock market where it was in late 1986 with no further consequences, recessionary or even depressionary.

7

The Next Recession Will Test Whether the World's Financial Structure Can Avoid a Depression

Recessions come in all sizes, shapes, and flavors, and the important question is, how long and deep will the next one be? The answer depends on how much protectionism and how many financial crises are spawned by it. These two problem areas have been successfully contained since they emerged as major threats five years ago, but during that five years, the world has enjoyed business expansion. The test will come during the next recession, and will determine whether that recession is a standard business correction or something much deeper.

During the next business slump, protectionist pressures will increase. Congress will look for a scapegoat, and foreigners who don't vote in U.S. elections will do very nicely in Congress's eyes. Furthermore, if as we believe the next recession is initiated by an agonizing reappraisal by consumers of their excessive borrowing and spending patterns, and a realization that the American dream of ever-increasing purchasing power is over for them, they, too, will be looking for a scapegoat. And they, too, will probably settle on foreigners, arguing that if they could only cut off those slave-labor-produced imports at the border they could go back to the lives they knew and loved. As discussed in Chapter 2, protectionism is ultimately deflationary and depressing to the world's economies.

The next recession also will intensify the myriad financial problems that arose in the 1970s, when many bet on inflation lasting forever, and invested heavily in commodities and other tangible assets on a highly leveraged basis. A global slowdown will reduce the demand for Third World exports and thereby the funds available to Latin American and other big debtor nations for debt servicing, increasing the likelihood of widespread defaults. U.S. agriculture is heavily dependent on exports and also will be in trouble in the next recession when Third World and other countries are too weak to continue buying American farm products. The problem is that productivity in U.S. agriculture grows faster than American caloric intake: we don't eat enough to keep up, and without export growth the industry shrinks. Overbuilt office buildings will also be in trouble. What companies will want to move into new, bigger, and more expensive space when they are trying to cut costs in a recession? Many leveraged buyouts will be in hot water, since they're in a deadly race between the start of the next recession and getting their debts paid down: whichever occurs first determines whether they're viable. Many probably won't be.

The Federal Reserve and other monetary authorities will continue to do everything they can to isolate and bail out these problem children one by one, dumping money out of airplanes if necessary. The risk is that the problems may come so thick and so fast as to overwhelm the monetary authorities. Then people will start to say "Who's next?" and confidence in the financial system will evaporate.

Third World Debt Problems -- Nearly Hopeless

Of particular concern is the Third World debt crisis. Led by Citicorp in May 1987, American banks set aside reserves to cover 25% of their loans to Third World debtors. In mid-December 1987, another round of reserve increases was initiated by Bank of Boston, which wrote off or reserved 63% of its nontrade-related Third World loans. Is the end in sight? Probably not.

In the inflationary 1970s, when commodity-exporting countries were being begged by banks to borrow money, they all did with gay abandon, but few invested the loan proceeds in productive resources that would generate the funds needed to service those debts. Convinced that commodity prices would rise forever, those countries used the money to import consumer goods or build hopeless steel mills and other projects that they thought would make them industrial powers overnight, or else, simply smuggled the funds abroad. Mexico, for example, bet the hacienda on crude oil prices reaching $100 per barrel when it borrowed massive amounts that were largely squandered. Consequently, even if the prices of their commodity exports had only stabilized, those countries would have been in difficult financial straits. Instead, the collapse of many commodity prices, and the switch of inflation-adjusted interest rates from negative to historically high levels, left them in deep, deep trouble.

Furthermore, new loans have dried up in recent years, so debt service and flight capital have transferred huge amounts of money -- about $30 billion in 1986 alone -- from Third World debtors to creditor countries. In Latin America, the transfer of funds has amounted to about 4% of GNP or about one quarter of domestic savings. In contrast, German reparation payments after World War I were only about 2.5% of GNP.

Compounding these problems is the decline in investment per capita in the developing countries. Capital formation has declined about 35% since 1980. Both foreign investors and local entrepreneurs have feared instability and higher taxes and have consequently moved their funds to safer locations.

These problems, of course, aren't new. Some of us talked about them over a decade ago when they were first developing. The Federal Reserve under Paul Volcker has been well aware of them but hoped to keep the current expansion going long enough for the banks to expand their other assets and capital. That way, when it finally became clear that the developing country loans were worth little, if anything, those debts would be small enough, in relative terms, that it wouldn't matter. But Brazil's default in 1987 cut short the financial community's hope for a painless solution and revealed the naked Emperor with all his warts. The inescapable fact is that essentially bankrupt Third World debtors owe $120 billion to U.S. banks, with Brazil accounting for $23.3 billion and Mexico for $23.5 billion.

In the spring of 1987, many hoped that the Citicorp-led round of 25% reserves against Third World loans would take care of the problem. After all, those loans were then selling in the secondary market at about 25% discounts to face value. But those prices were really inflated. Many of the sales were among banks, as money center banks bought out regionals who wanted out and could otherwise embarrass the big banks who induced them to make the loans in the first place. Others were between banks that wanted to diversify their portfolios. One heavy in, say, Argentine loans might have traded with one that was up to its eyeballs in Brazilian loans. It's like changing deck chairs on the Titanic!

Furthermore, after the round of 25% reserves against Third World loans, the finance ministers of many of the countries involved told the U.S. banks in effect that "You are assuming that only 75% of our loans are good. We're taking you at your word, and therefore only plan to service that amount." The banks were not happy about this, of course, but the net result was a further precipitous decline in the value of Third World loans in the secondary market. Argentine loans, for example, had been selling at a 30% discount to face value before the Citicorp announcement, but then fell to a 35% discount.

The process will probably continue, with Third World debtors planning to service no more than 50% of their debts since so many banks followed Bank of Boston, as shown in FIGURE 16. Other banks that have added to reserves or written off more Third World loans include Mellon Bank Corp., First Wisconsin, Midlantic Corp., Huntington Bancshares, Inc., and Indiana National Corporation. AmSouth Bancorp sold $22 million in loans to Central and South American nations at about a 50% discount, and charged off an additional $9.9 million in Latin American loans. Its only remaining Latin American loans are $5 million in trade obligations insured by U.S. government agencies.

FIGURE 16

PERCENTAGES OF NONTRADE THIRD WORLD
LOANS WRITTEN OFF OR RESERVED

American Express Bank	60%
Bank of Boston	63
Continental Illinois Corp.	50
First Chicago Corp.	56
First Interstate Bancorp	53
First Wachovia Corp.	60
National Westminster Bank USA	35
NCNB Corp.	56*
Security Pacific Corp.	54
Wells Fargo & Co.	48

* Wrote off 56% of Mexican loans.
Sold all civilian loans in 1986,
and all Argentine loans in 1987:III.

Not all banks with substantial Third World loans have followed Bank of Boston's lead, because many large money center banks simply don't have enough capital to withstand additional reserves or writeoffs of their substantial Third World loan portfolios. FIGURE 17 shows that Manufacturers Hanover, Bank of America, Chase Manhattan, and Citicorp all have loans to Mexico, Brazil, Argentina, Venezuela, and Chile that equalled more than 100% of their equity capital at the end of 1986. In contrast, Security Pacific, which did take the additional reserves, had only a 49% exposure.

Separating the Sheep from the Goats

To reach 50% of reserves against Third World loans, Bank of America would need to set aside more than $3 billion in additional reserves, Manufacturers Hanover and Chase Manhattan more than $2 billion additional, and Bankers Trust, J.P. Morgan and Company, and Chemical New York Corp. about $1 billion additional each. Obviously, none of these banks has announced additional reserves or writeoffs, nor has Bank of New York Company. In effect, the sheep -- the strongly capitalized regional banks with few bad international loans -- are being sepa-

FIGURE 17

BANKS' EXPOSURE IN MEXICO, BRAZIL, ARGENTINA, VENEZUELA, AND CHILE (1986)

	Exposure	% of Equity
Manufacturers Hanover Trust	$7.5 bil.	199%
Bank of America	7.6	188
Chase Manhattan	7.0	143
Citicorp	10.4	114
Security Pacific	1.4	49

SOURCES: IBCA, Inc., Barron's

rated from the goats -- the money center banks with Third World loans too big to reserve against or write off. Regional banks are not only flexing their financial muscles and widening the gap by taking additional reserves and writeoffs, maybe even baiting the money center banks and daring them to follow -- but they are also simply exiting the Third World loan business, thereby eliminating the possibility of being called upon to come up with their "fair share" of the next round of new loans to those debtors or loans to capitalize overdue and unpayable interest.

Comes the Recession . . .

As bad as Third World debtor positions are, they developed over five years in which the world has enjoyed economic expansion. A recent study by the World Bank points out that the world's debtor nations owed $1.19 trillion at the end of 1987, and are expected to owe even more -- $1.245 trillion at the end of 1988. The World Bank observes that "in the five years since 1982, no country involved in rescheduling its debts has significantly reduced its debt ratios. The trend has strayed in the opposite direction." Furthermore, last year the debtor countries paid $29 billion more in repayments than they received in new loans -- capital continues to flow out of these struggling developing nations.

The World Bank goes on: "What is particularly worrying is that the adjustment has proved so difficult in a period of expansion for industrial countries that is already one of the longest on record. What would be the chances for a solution during a recession?" Furthermore, the Bank observes that the long period of no progress on the problem has led to a sort of "debt fatigue." My dad always says that you can stand anything for a little while, even hanging. The problem is that both lenders and Third World borrowers have hanged too long.

Mexico to the Rescue?

Some believe that the new plan to convert part of Mexico's debt into new Mexican bonds backed by zero-coupon U.S. Treasury obligations offers a way out of the crisis, or at least a partial solution. Under this plan, not yet implemented as of this writing, Mexico will issue up to $10 billion in new bonds in return for about twice that amount in outstanding bank loans to Mexico. This would, in effect, allow Mexico to cancel part of its $100 billion in foreign debt, $78 billion of it owed to foreign banks, including $24 billion to U.S. institutions.

This plan does have advantages. It's certainly better than the recent scheme in which Brazil put up $1.5 billion, the banks put up $3.0 billion, and then they counted the $4.5 billion total as interest payments to the banks -- capitalization of interest in its crudest form! Also, by in effect cancelling some loans, Mexico increases its chances for servicing the remainder even though the interest rate on the new bonds exceeds that on the loans they will replace.

But, the problem is that the U.S. Treasury zero-coupon bonds back only the principal of the Mexican bonds, and not the interest payments. As a result, the Mexican government will support the new bonds with only $2 billion in zero-coupon Treasury obligations -- the present value of $10 billion when they mature 20 years hence.

In effect, banks would be trading about $20 billion in Mexican loans for $10 billion in the new Mexican bonds backed by U.S. Treasury zero-coupon bonds now worth only $2 billion. The remaining $8 billion depends on the

Mexicans' ability to meet the interest payments. This is highly questionable, if, as we expect, a global recession develops and the oil price, and with it, Mexico's ability to generate foreign exchange, collapses. Banks would be better off, we believe, to sell their Mexican loans on the open market even if they take a 60% discount. But then, we're back to the problem of whether that discount won't be even greater later, especially if a worldwide recession develops and oil prices plummet.

What's to be Done?

What's the ultimate resolution of the Third World debt crisis? Possible solutions, including debt-for-equity swaps, are inadequate to deal with the problem, and in the final analysis, the U.S. government may be forced to help if -- although more likely, when -- other borrowers follow Ecuador, Peru, and Brazil into default. The government could take over the bank loans directly, but the impact on the federal budget deficit would probably be unacceptable. Nor is the public reaction to what will appear to be a bailout of the banks politically desirable. More likely is the approach used with failing thrifts in this country. Accounting rules would be changed so that the difference between the actual and face value of the developing country loans would be treated as goodwill and written off over long enough periods so as to avoid wiping out the banks' equity, perhaps over 40 or 50 years.

Oil Prices -- Down Again?

Another ominous sign of financial difficulties is the likelihood of a further big decline in oil prices. As we pointed out in The World Has Definitely Changed, keeping oil prices anywhere near current levels requires continuing success by the OPEC cartel. However, excess inventories and the all-but-declared shooting war between Saudi Arabia and Iran are straining the cartel. The Saudis once again show signs of being unwilling to cut their own production so others, in this case their enemy Iran, can expand production without fear of destroying the price structure. The Saudi government's recent borrowings in international markets to fund its budget deficit indicates the extent of pressure on its economy. And, with a recession or worse in the offing, OPEC will probably not be able to control oil prices.

If OPEC again is unable or unwilling to cut production enough to sustain prices in the $18-$20-per-barrel range, how low can oil prices fall, especially in a recessionary environment? A possible floor is the cost of producing oil in the Middle East, or about 50¢ to $3 per barrel. This sounds ridiculously low, but as prices decline, production increases as financially weak exporters in and out of OPEC produce and export more, not less, oil, to get the same number of dollars to service their huge foreign debts. This increased output in turn further reduces prices, leading to more production, etc., in a spiral of disequilibrium. OPEC failed to prevent a huge price decline in early 1986, and each time it tries to get its members to support prices, and fails, it is harder to get cooperation in the future, and the urge by financially weak producers to cheat and to export more increases.

Another Oil Price Collapse -- A Net Negative for the World

But isn't this all good for the world, in the final analysis? After all, when oil prices began rising in 1973, it was bad news for every country except the OPEC producers and a handful of other oil exporters. An oil price collapse would obviously reduce inflationary pressures, as well as the big trade balance problems for many less-developed countries that lack domestic energy production.

The negatives of the world price collapse, however, far outweigh the positives. An oil price decline is simply not symmetrical with an oil price increase, since the world, including the OPEC countries, has adapted to high oil prices in the last decade. Most OPEC countries, with the exception of the sparsely populated Persian Gulf sheikdoms, have spent all their revenues and more, and are now heavily in debt. Even Saudi Arabia is now borrowing. Many non-OPEC exporters are in the same boat. Mexico, among the world's largest debtors, is an extreme but not unique example.

While oil prices create enormous difficulties for financially weak producers who depend almost entirely on oil for their imports, the benefits for such Third World importers as Brazil and the Philippines are less impressive, since oil imports comprise only a fraction of those countries' total imports.

Some have adapted to higher oil prices in ways that could be difficult to reverse. Brazil has developed a sizable gasohol industry that would be wiped out by a collapse in oil prices. More important, even if the effects of the oil- and non-oil-producing countries were the same, the pluses and minuses could not be netted against each other. If an oil price collapse succeeded in pulling the Philippines a mile away from the financial precipice but pushed Venezuela over the edge and onto the rocks a mile below, the two positions could not be combined so that the two countries would still, on average, be standing on the edge of that cliff!

Is Another Depression Possible?

The possibility that the next recession may create serious protectionism and financial crises, particularly with the stock market crash now behind us, suggests the risk of a 1930s-style depression. As discussed in Chapter 24, "Depression Is More Likely Than Many May Think," of our book, The World Has Definitely Changed, "the parallels between the world now and that of the late 1920s are indeed frightening, and the possibilities that a 1930s-style depression occurs cannot be completely ruled out." These parallels include:

A. Like in the late 1920s and the 1930s, there are now worldwide surpluses of almost everything.

B. Then and now, soaring inflation has given way to deflation in a number of industrial and agricultural commodities, as well as farmland and other forms of real estate.

C. Then and now, deflation in commodity prices and weak demand has made it impossible for many countries with huge debts to meet their obligations.

D. Protectionism was a dominant force in the 1920s and 1930s and is now.

E. In both periods, no nation is a dominant enough world leader to control protectionist pressures and financial crises.

F. U.S. agriculture was in terrible shape in the late 1920s and 1930s. This time, agriculture, mining, energy, and manufacturing have been devastated by fierce international competition and inadequate global demand.

G. In the late 1920s and from the early 1980s until recently, financial markets were booming. FIGURE 18 * shows the frighteningly close parallel to the Dow Jones Industrial Average, complete with the crashes in 1929 and October 1987. Moreover, greed was so great that insider trading was a problem in both eras.

H. A flattening in purchasing power for middle-income Americans occurred for over a decade before both the 1929 stock market crash and the 1987 Crash. The lack of middle-income income growth contributed to the lack of spending in the Depression, and may again.

I. Money velocity, the ratio of money to GNP, fell rapidly in the 1920s and in the 1980s, indicating that Federal Reserve monetary policy was tighter than the credit authorities realized. Furthermore, despite the stock market crash on October 19, 1987, the Fed still appears to be fighting the last war, inflation and the weak dollar, and not the next, global deflation. Similarly, in the early 1930s, the Fed fought the previous war, excessive stock speculation of the late 1920s.

* Just for fun -- or tears -- compare this graph with the way it looked in early 1986, before the Crash, as shown on page 136 of The World Has Definitely Changed -- when the parallel was ominous, but not yet fully convincing to many.

FIGURE 18

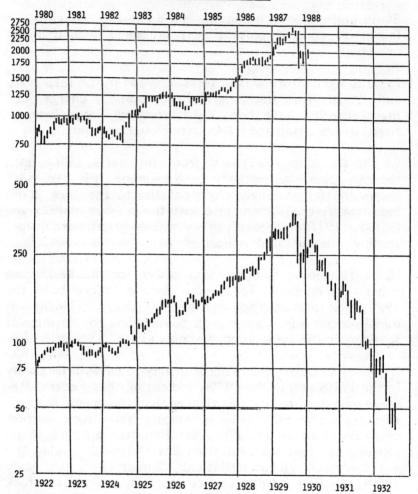

What About All Those Safeguards?

Furthermore, as we noted in The World Has Definitely Changed, "Even some of the factors that are supposed to be quite different from the late 1920s, and are meant to protect the financial system from collapse, are not really that different:

A. The Securities and Exchange Commission, created in reaction to the 1929 stock market crash and the Depression that followed, carefully regulates stock markets and prevents excessive margin debt. But, speculative risks now can just as easily be taken with options, futures contracts, and junk bonds as they were with highly leveraged stocks in the 1920s. . . . Furthermore, index mutual funds engaged in arbitrage trading can completely circumvent the rules designed to prevent a cumulative stock market collapse through selling stocks short.

B. The built-in fiscal stabilizers are now expected to cushion any weakness in the private sector. If the economy starts to slip, corporate and individual tax payments automatically become smaller while government spending on social security, unemployment benefits, etc. rises. The resulting increase in the federal deficit ostensibly offsets the weakness in the private sector.

But, the Gramm-Rudman law actually reverses this process and makes fiscal policy destabilizing. The law requires government spending cuts or revenue increases equal to the amount by which the budget deficit exceeds the specified target level. But the weaker the economy, the higher the estimated budget deficit from which the Gramm-Rudman cuts must be made, the bigger the cuts in spending or the increases in taxes needed to reach the law's deficit targets, the more the economy is depressed, and so it goes in a potential downward spiral.

The federal government had a budget surplus in 1929, but with the onset of the Depression, it turned to deficits beginning in 1930. The reaction was not to accept this as a built-in stabilizer working the way it was supposed to, but to raise taxes to restore fiscal integrity. Now, of course, we're starting out with a very large federal budget deficit, but the reaction is the same.

Many in and out of Washington believe that the lack of control of the federal deficit had a lot to do with the recent stock market crash, and that calamity scared Washington into serious work on the budget problem. But as noted in Chapter 6, the budget compromise hammered out between Congress and the Administration was inadequate to restore confidence in stocks or reduce interest rates substantially, so the net effect is simply to reduce demand in a world, like that of the early 1930s, that desperately needs more, not less, demand.

C. Deposit insurance by the FDIC for banks and by the FSLIC for thrift institutions was also introduced in reaction to the Depression, but it is not as risk-free as it may appear. Americans still seem to love risks, and when the government raises the safety net, people climb to a higher perch from which to take that half-mile dive into a wet sponge! People throughout the country are now depositing funds in any financial institution that pays high rates of interest, regardless of its financial health, as long as it has federal insurance coverage.

Recent history shows that the institutions paying the highest rates are the closest to bankruptcy.

We continue to believe that the probability of a 1930s-type depression is only in the 10%-20% range, but the consequences are so significant that it cannot be ignored in anyone's business plan or portfolio strategy.

8

The Kondratieff Wave
Is Right on Schedule

Despite the similarities with the late 1920s and early
1930s just mentioned in Chapter 7, we do believe that the
probability of a 1930s-style Depression is in the relatively low 10%-to-20% range. More likely is a deep recession
followed by a sluggish recovery and perhaps several more
serious recessions as the many financial and economic imbalances in the world's economic and financial structure
are gradually worked out. This pattern describes a Kondratieff wave depression of the sort that this country
suffered in the 1830s and 1840s and again in the 1880s and
1890s -- periods of deep recessions and weak recoveries --
as opposed to the collapse of the 1930s, which was also a
Kondratieff wave depression.

What Sort of Depression is Likely?

As described in our earlier book, Is Inflation Ending? Are
You Ready?, written in the summer of 1982 and published
in 1983:

> The Kondratieff wave is named after the Russian
> economist Nikolai Kondratieff, who correctly pre-
> dicted big problems for the capitalist countries in the
> 1930s. But he made a strategic blunder by suggesting
> that the capitalist world would survive. The reaction
> of the Russians was predictable, and Kondratieff spent
> the rest of his career in Siberia.

The Kondratieff wave holds that capitalist countries have consistently been subject to a 50-to 60-year cycle of extended growth and decline, commodity price peaks and troughs, and rising and falling interest rates. After studying more than 100 years of data on commodity prices in industrialized countries, Kondratieff found that after a long period of expansion, approximately 24 years, a long decline ensued, lasting anywhere from 23 to 35 years. Kondratieff described the wave this way:

> The upswing of the first long wave embraces the period from 1789 to 1814, i.e., 25 years; its decline begins in 1814 and ends in 1849, a period of 35 years. The cycle is, therefore, completed in 60 years.

> The rise of the second wave begins in 1849 and ends in 1873, lasting 24 years. . . . The decline of the second wave begins in 1873 and ends in 1896, a period of 23 years. The length of the second wave is 47 years.

> The upward movement of the third wave begins in 1896 and ends in 1920, its duration being 24 years. The decline of the wave, according to all data, begins in 1920.*

If one assumes a typical down wave lasting 23 to 35 years, the fourth up cycle probably began in the late 1940s or early 1950s, precisely when the postwar economic and stock market boom started. If we arbitrarily pick 1950 as the year the postwar economic expansion began, then 24 years of economic growth would put the next peak in 1974. It is ominous, to say the least, that the worst recession in 30 years struck in 1974, accompanied by sharply declining stock and commodity prices.

* The Long Waves in Economic Life, Readings in Business Cycle Theory, American Economic Association, Blakiston, Philadelphia, 1944.

Actually, many people who were only slightly familiar with the long wave thought that 1974 was the beginning of another depression, based on Kondratieff's theory. But a strict interpretation of the long wave indicates that a gradual plateau exists for eight to ten years before the depression actually occurs.

Indeed, Kondratieff divided the economic decline into two phases: a primary plateau followed by a decade or so of gradual decline, which he called "secondary prosperity," and then a depression. His work showed a peak in 1814 and a gradually declining plateau through 1819, a peak after the Civil War and a gradually declining plateau for 10 years and a peak in 1920, with the great depression beginning nine years later.

Adding 8 or 10 years to 1974, we get 1982 or 1984 as the likely target date for the beginning of the next depression.

We may have been a bit early in our dating for the next Kondratieff wave depression, but the similarity between the typical decline phase and the depression part of it, and recent developments is both striking and growing:

1. The decline phase is initiated by an unpopular war -- the War of 1812, the Civil War, World War I, and most recently the Vietnam War -- that starts out with the pursuit of some great cause at the end of the upswing, when confidence is at its height, but ends with nothing but disillusionment.

2. Those unpopular wars are followed by a surge in commodity prices and then weakness for the balance of the downswing. This happened after the War of 1812, the Civil War, and World War I. The surge after the end of the Vietnam War and peaking in the early 1980s is right on schedule.

3. Protectionism occurs during the depression part of the decline phase when global supplies of almost

everything far exceed demand. The McKinley Tariff Act of 1890, the Wilson tariff of 1894, and the Kingley tariff of 1897 were all blatantly protectionist, and so, of course, was the notorious Smoot-Hawley Tariff Act of 1930 at the beginning of the next depression. Growing protectionist sentiments today are heading in the same direction.

4. The decade long period of gradual decline, or "secondary prosperity" begins with a severe inventory correction which is the deepest recession of the upswing -- the 1920-21 slump, for example -- and is followed by a decade in which people believe that all is well -- "the Roaring 20s." The mid-1970s inventory collapse and the following decade are very similar.

5. Agriculture is particularly hard hit during the down phase, and farmland prices collapse before the correction in other forms of real estate. This time the agricultural depression and the oil patch collapse started in the early 1980s. Will the rest of real estate follow?

6. Political scandals, at least in this country, occur at the beginning of the down phase of the Kondratieff wave. Grant's second term was scandal ridden, Harding's Administration suffered numerous corruption problems including the Teapot Dome scandal, and Nixon resigned under fire as a result of Watergate.

7. When the down phase starts, the old technologies that drove the previous upswing are fully exploited and overbuilt. The technologies that will drive the next upswing are already known, but not commercially exploited to a great degree.

This offers one explanation of the Kondratieff wave. The upswing is driven by the surge of investment in new technologies -- canals and river boats in the early 1800s, railroads in the 1850-1870 period, autos in the early twentieth century, and basic industries and construction in the first three decades after World War II.

Then, investment in these areas gets so excessive that it declines, and the economy falters since the investment in the next technology isn't big enough yet to move overall business activity. The result is the down phase of the wave. For example, railroads were developed in the early 19th century, but did not become major economic driving forces until the the middle of the century. At present, as noted in Chapter 4, many high technologies are already developed, but investment in them is not yet big enough to offset faltering basic industries and construction. Later, however, high-tech investment should grow large enough to drive the next upswing. In effect then, the down phase of the wave is the gap between the full exploitation of one technology and the onset of massive investment in the next.

There is another simpler explanation of the 50-year Kondratieff wave that may sound whimsical, but seems to us like an attack of common sense. Human nature changes very slowly over time, if at all. Therefore, people with similar background experiences react to like circumstances in similar ways. Since it takes about 50 years for everyone who remembers the last trip through the meat grinder to die or retire, only after that length of time are people likely to repeat their mistakes. How about the 1987 stock market crash as a case in point? Check back to FIGURE 18 on page 56 to note the similarities between the market action leading up to it and that preceding the 1929 Crash 58 years earlier.

In the aftermath of the 1987 Crash, it's clear that it wasn't the margin requirements and other safeguards introduced in the 1930s that prevented rampant stock market speculation and a stock market collapse from occurring between the 1930s and the 1980s. Rather, it was the vast number of still-active brokers and investors who remembered the 1929 experience indelibly. Once they were dead or out to pasture, human ingenuity took over and developed stock options, futures contracts, and myriad other techniques for circumventing those earlier safeguards. American ingenuity, driven by greed and deprived of fear has no trouble in overcoming mere laws and regulations.

The world may avoid another Kondratieff wave depression, but we're certainly keeping our eyes on the historical patterns. So far the parallels are intriguing and frightening. In any event, perhaps the best way to estimate the depth and structure of any upcoming depression is simply to average the three that the nation has been through so far. This mathematical exercise points to a depression like in the 1830s and 1840s or in the 1880s and 1890s which consisted of a series of deep recessions and weak recoveries, as opposed to the all-out collapse of the 1930s.

The result of this averaging approach is a key rationale for our putting the odds of a 1930s-style Depression at only 10%-20% -- although the consequences if it does occur are so significant that it cannot be ignored in anyone's business plan or portfolio strategy. (Neither can a series of deep recessions interspersed by weak recoveries, for that matter.) The low odds decidedly do not reflect any acceptance on our part of the idea that a rerun of the 1930s is impossible because everyone now is so much smarter and governments know so much more about how to manipulate the economy, that trouble can be avoided.

Eye of the Hurricane?

Quite to the contrary, the rather blase general attitude toward the Crash of October 1987, in and out of Wall Street, despite the huge and numerous financial and economic imbalances around the globe, has an eerie resemblance to the attitudes after the 1929 Crash, and suggests that people are no smarter now than then. Like then, we may be in the eye of the hurricane. We've come through the wall of wind and rain of the Crash, and are in the calm sea-blue sky area where all looks well. But, there just may be an even more dangerous deluge on the other side that we will have to endure as the hurricane moves toward us.

The consensus certainly thought all was well in late 1929 and early 1930 despite the fact that a recession was already in evidence. Business in the U.S. peaked in

August 1929 -- actually two months ahead of the stock market, and by January 1930, industrial production was 11.1% off its peak, new orders for durable goods were down 13.8%, and building contracts had fallen 40%. Despite initial rosy reports of Christmas sales in 1929:IV, consumer spending fell at a 17.3% annual rate, and private construction plummeted 41.3%.

Still, The New York Times, in its December 31, 1929, edition was so relaxed about the Crash and the economy that it named Commander Richard Byrd's expedition to the South Pole as the outstanding news event of 1929. Furthermore, as an interesting review of the period in the January 2, 1988, London Financial Times points out, in January 1930, the National Economic League, an organization of business and civic leaders, polled its member on "the paramount problems for the United States in 1930." Heading the list were Administration of Justice, Prohibition, Lawlessness, Crime, and Law Enforcement. Organized crime certainly held people's attention back then! Unemployment was eighteenth on their list, yet it had already risen from 750,000 in September 1929 to 3 million at the beginning of 1930, and would reach 7 million by the end of the year.

The economic weakness was viewed as merely a cyclical inventory correction, and The New York Times stated that business cycles were becoming "less violent," as government policies improved, the Federal Reserve stabilized the financial system, and businesses increased the sophistication of their planning. President Hoover made his infamous statement that "the fundamental business of America is sound."

Just as many in America's heartland today snicker about how the Wall Street yuppies got what was coming to them with the October 1987 Crash, many in 1929 had the same attitude toward stock market speculators. Individual stockholders were such a tiny minority of the population in 1929 that their activity hardly seemed relevant to the economy, and pension fund stock holding was virtually unknown. In view of what followed the 1929 Crash, it's hardly comforting to note that individual stockholders comprised only about 1% of American families at that time compared with 20% today, when stocks dominate many pension fund portfolios as well.

Like this time around, many in 1929 even thought that the Crash was a return to sanity and "normalcy," to use the 1920s term. These included Henry Ford, President Hoover, and H.C. Hopson, head of Associated Gas and Electric, who said it was "undoubtedly beneficial to the business interests of the country to have the gambling type of speculator eliminated." The Commercial and Financial Chronicle had vehemently opposed the stock speculation of the late 1920s and described the earlier soaring market as "a nightmare from which the country has been happily delivered."

Those who believe that the Federal Reserve, which raised the discount rate in August 1987 but then bailed out Wall Street after the October 19 debacle, acted much more intelligently this time than in 1929 should examine the record. In August 1929 the Fed raised the discount rate, at last, to calm the stock market speculation, but after the October 1929 Crash, the Fed cut that rate and pumped money into the system. In fact, George Harrison, then president of the Federal Reserve Bank of New York, had his Bank buy $160 million in Treasury securities the week of the Crash to bail out Wall Street brokerage houses, vastly exceeding his legal weekly limit of $25 million.

Even President Hoover wasn't as dumb as he's remembered -- and since the federal government ran a budget surplus in 1929, there was leeway to offset the weakening economy with fiscal stimulus that is lacking in today's high deficit climate. In November 1929, President Hoover called for tax cuts and expanded public works programs. He also gathered the captains of industry and made them promise to help sustain purchasing power by maintaining wage levels and increasing capital spending. After that meeting, Henry Ford raised the wages of his auto workers from his celebrated $5 per day to $7 per day. Nevertheless, the average hourly wage of those production workers lucky enough to keep their jobs in manufacturing fell 21% from 1929 to 1932, and since hours were cut as well, average weekly earnings fell 32%. Many weren't so lucky. By 1932, 38% of those production jobs in manufacturing that existed in 1929 had been eliminated.

Maybe there's no rerun of the 1930s Depression or even a serious recession ahead, but don't get too relaxed just because it hasn't appeared yet! As Damon Runyon, taking off on Ecclesiastes, said, "It may not be that the race is always to the swift, nor the battle to the strong. But that's the way to bet!"

9

A Depression Is More Likely
in Japan
than in the U.S.

Ask most people which industrial economy today is the strongest, and they will answer, Japan. Yet if any are to experience serious financial problems and a depression in coming years, Japan is the most likely. In many ways, Japan today is where the U.S. was in the late 1920s -- the emerging world power, but still about to experience some difficult financial and economic crises.

The U.S. and the U.K. in the 1920s -- A Leadership Shift

The 1920s was an era in which global economic leadership was shifting from the U.K. to the U.S. World War I ended Britain's world domination, which began in the latter half of the eighteenth century. After Europe recovered from World War I, global excess supply conditions reigned, and the U.K. suffered nonstop double-digit unemployment rates in the 1920s. In this environment, deflation was the rule, and even after U.K. consumer prices declined by one quarter in the 1920-21 inventory recession, prices declined another 8.9% between 1922 and 1929. Real GNP in Britain rose a meager 13% between 1922 and 1929, and huge trade deficits averaging about 8% of GNP were seen in those years. In short, the U.K. was a weakening economy that was living off of its earlier immense foreign investments. Stock prices rose from 1921 to 1929, but reflecting all these problems, the increase was only 87% compared to the much larger 497% increase in the U.S.

The mantle of a world leader was passing to the U.S., but this country was reluctant to accept it. Isolationism held sway here until World War II. During World War I, U.S. agriculture and manufacturing capacity expanded tremendously in order to supply war-torn Europe. This left America with excess supply problems when Europe revived in the 1920s, but the problems were much less severe than in the U.K. and were covered up by the roaring 1920s. The U.S. unemployment rate averaged 3.7% in the 1922-29 period. Deflation was felt, but to a lesser extent than in Britain. The CPI declined 16% in the 1920-21 inventory recession, and a further 2% between 1922 and 1929. Real GNP was robust, and rose almost 40% during those years, and the U.S. was running consistent trade surpluses -- not as large as during World War I, but still over 1% of GNP. And, beginning with World War I, the U.S. became a net lender to the world.

U.S. Becomes Reluctant Leader in 1920s

Securities markets in the 1920s recognized what Americans were reluctant to accept politically: that this country was fast becoming the world economic leader. Money flowed into the U.S. stock market, and prices soared as the Dow Jones Industrial Average rose almost sixfold from its low in 1921 to its peak in 1929. Aiding and abetting this rush into stocks were the low interest rates at the time. After World War I, the U.K. had reestablished the prewar price of gold in sterling terms, thereby overvaluing sterling. In order to prevent a massive flight of funds to New York, the Federal Reserve held down U.S. interest rates. This encouraged stock investment by discouraging bond ownership, and made borrowing to speculate in stocks very attractive. Furthermore, the only margin requirements then were set by brokerage houses and banks, and they often amounted to no more than 10%-15% of a stock's price.

Then things became unglued. The U.S. stock market fell 89% in terms of the Dow Jones Industrial Average between 1929 and 1932, dropping below the 1921 low. The CPI declined 24% in the 1929-33 years and real GNP fell 22%. The ratio of the value of the New York Stock Exchange stocks to GNP was cut in half, declining from 70% in 1928 to 35% in 1931.

The excess capacity created to feed and supply war-torn Europe in World War I was certainly revealed after the roaring 1920s ended, and it finally took rearmament in Europe and the U.S., and World War II itself, to use it up.

Stocks had not gone to such extremes in the U.K. in the 1920s, but they still fell about one quarter in value. This clearly reflected a depressed British economy, and real GNP declined about 25% in the 1929-32 period. Consumer prices in the U.K. fell another 14% during those years.

Now It's the U.S. and Japan

The relationship between the U.S. and Japan now is very similar to that between the U.K. and the U.S. 60 years ago. The U.S. was the global economic leader from World War II to the mid-1960s. By then, Europe and Japan had been rebuilt, and had become our rivals. Furthermore, America dissipated its strength on the Vietnam War and unproductive Great Society programs in the 1960s.

In the early 1980s, high inflation ended and commodity prices collapsed, and the world moved rapidly from shortages to surpluses. The U.S. has been the world's high-cost producer in many industries for years, but the shortages of the 1970s hid this fact. With the surpluses of the 1980s, however, it stood out like a sore thumb, despite the decline in the dollar. This inability to compete internationally, coupled with our zeal to consume, has led to huge trade deficits, which reached 3.7% of GNP in 1987. The borrowing to finance those ongoing trade deficits has reversed 70 years of U.S. net lending, and in 1987 this country became a net international debtor. Not surprisingly, many American jobs have been exported.

. . . With Japan Reluctant to Take the Lead

Cost cutting by American business does show great promise for reviving our international competitiveness, and some attention is being given to government spending and deficits. Nevertheless, the U.S. is starting from a pretty deep hole, especially compared with the Japanese. In many ways Japan is now the natural world leader, but like the U.S. in the interwar period, it is reluctant to accept the responsibility either economically or militarily. Japan developed a phenomenally strong trade surplus of $90 billion in fiscal 1987, which ended March 31, up from $53 billion in fiscal 1986. Even after accounting for the rapid increase in the yen against the dollar, the trade surplus rose between those two years. Not surprisingly Japan has, perhaps reluctantly, become the world's key lender in recent years.

Japan's Speculative Markets

This environment has led to a dynamic Japanese stock market, and even though it was affected as the 1987 Crash in the U.S. spread, it has recovered much more than the U.S. market. The total value of all Japanese equity markets is now larger than the total of U.S. markets, but, with the Japanese economy only half as big as that of the U.S., the ratio of market value to GNP in Japan is more than twice that in the U.S. The market value of one stock, Nippon Telegraph & Telephone, exceeds the entire German stock market's value. The Japanese real estate market also has been highly speculative, with prices now at almost unbelievably high levels.

The Japanese stock and real estate markets will probably suffer substantial and recession-triggering corrections, sooner or later. And, a collapse in the Japanese stock market could well have global repercussions as the Japanese would view it as a loss of national face and do everything, including selling foreign stock and bond holdings, to shore up their sagging stocks. It is clear that Japanese leaders get very upset at the thought of extreme weakness in their stock market. During the market slump of the mid-1960s, the government actually bought stocks to shore it up. The margin requirements were cut immediately when stocks dipped in the summer of 1987 in order to make it easier to buy stocks.

... Shored Up by Government Buying Pressure

The day after the October 19, 1987 Crash on Wall Street, the Japanese Finance Ministry met with that nation's four largest brokers and encouraged them to come to grips with the panic. Aggressive sales campaigns ensued, and the next day the Nikkei index soared 9.3%, making up for more than half of the previous day's 14.9% plunge. A week later, the Finance Ministry also met with the three major Japanese trust banks and three leading life insurance companies, again to urge them to buy stocks aggressively.

The sizeable Japanese holdings of American stocks and bonds would, of course, be vulnerable to Japanese attempts, probably unsuccessful, to reverse a collapse in their stock market, and wholesale selling could trigger further major corrections in U.S. security prices. Furthermore, the question of how the ongoing U.S. federal deficit would be financed without Japanese participation would arise quickly, and a sharp sell off in the dollar could ensue. Those developments would probably feed on themselves, leading to further weakness in American stocks, bonds, and the dollar.

Problems for the U.S. financial markets could in turn trigger a recession here if this country isn't already in one, and with Japan and the U.S., the two largest economies in the free world, in recession or worse, the rest of the globe would soon follow. In this mess, the U.S. would probably look like the best of a bad lot to investors around the world, and their rush back to the U.S. would cause the dollar to rebound. Furthermore, a worldwide slump would easily kill the inflationary fears, as it would vividly remind everyone that the world continues to have surpluses of almost everything. As a result, U.S. interest rates would no doubt drop to even lower levels than before the whole gyration started.

Can the Japanese Economy Falter?

The Japanese stock and real estate markets may be vulnerable, but what about the Japanese economy, that bastion of postwar strength? That nation may be the next global economic leader, but like the U.S. in the 1930s, it still could go through a very rough period of transition because global conditions have changed, compared with what allowed rapid growth in Japan in the earlier postwar period. First, Japan was then the low-cost exporter; now it's the NICs that are chasing Japan up the scale of sophistication as they advance from exporting textiles to steel and ships, and now to consumer electronics and autos. As noted in Chapter 3, these countries link their currencies to the dollar and hence have become even cheaper producers while the yen's strength is hampering Japanese exports.

Despite Japan's resolve, it's far from obvious that that country can find enough areas of even more complex products to maintain its export-led growth. High-tech equipment is the next logical area in which to move, and one in which Japan is already heavily involved with. But excess capacity worldwide may hold down investment in this equipment for some time.

Secondly, Japan was able to emulate Western technology in the earlier postwar decades. Its manufacturers were the great imitators, developing products quickly by copying and improving what had been done in the U.S. and Europe. Now Japan has fully caught up, and develop its own new technologies -- a much more expensive process than to copy somebody else's.

Third, Japan earlier targeted industries in which it wanted to move, and did so at a time when there was such rapid growth that it didn't have to push existing companies aside in order to get a toehold. In autos, for example, Detroit didn't seem to know what was happening for at least a decade, even though Japan was gaining a significant market position in this country. Demand for autos was growing rapidly enough that Detroit still gained in dollar sales, even though it was losing market share. Now, in a world of surpluses, when Japan moves into an industry it has to shoulder out existing participants. This happened recently in the U.S. semiconductor industry where in order to gain a foothold, Japan had to push aside companies like Motorola and Texas Instruments. They reacted immediately, touching off a semiconductor trade war between Washington and Tokyo.

Protectionism, Strong Yen Will Hinder Efforts

Fourth, Japan now has a very strong yen to hinder its exports. And fifth, growing protectionism in the U.S. and Europe, primarily aimed at Japan, is also a problem for that economy, which for years has been almost entirely dependent on exports for economic growth. In reaction to protectionism and the strong yen, Japan is rapidly moving production to North America and Europe, and also to the NICs. This, however, not only creates unemployment at home but risks dissipating Japan's technical superiority in a number of industries. In 1982, Japanese manufacturing firms' overseas production stood at 3.4% of their domestic output, but by the year 2000 Japan's economic planning agency expects the ratio to jump to 20%.

All this does not suggest that Japan is finished -- any more than the U.S. was in the 1930s -- but that the country could have a rough road ahead. Japan is filled with very dedicated, competent people who undoubtedly will succeed, but they must make two traumatic transitions. First, they will have to move from an export-led to a domestically driven economy. They've started down that road, but despite government admonitions, it will be difficult to reorient their economy to domestic consumer spending and to investment in roads, schools, sewers, and other domestic areas, given the "export-or-die" mentality -- a state of mind that goes back at least to the Meiji restoration, which began in 1868.

Shifting to a World of Surpluses

Second, Japan probably must shift from a very rapidly growing economy to a more moderately growing one in a world of surpluses. This means changing a number of Japanese institutions, including lifetime employment, which is already fading in industries such as basic steel, but still covers one third of Japanese workers. It make sense in periods of strong growth, when more workers are always needed, but not when growth is slow and recessions lead to actual economic declines. Furthermore, the Japanese business practice of striving for market share with the assurance that adequate profitability will follow is logical in conditions of rapid expansion and surging market penetration, but could be disastrous in a world of surpluses and slow demand growth. In addition, a strong producer may be king in times of shortages, but when supply is excessive the regal role shifts to the consumer.

Also, the very low capitalization ratios prevalent in Japan for industrial corporations and financial institutions don't make much sense in a period when growth is anything but straight up. Capitalization ratios will probably need to be increased, even though the Japanese business structure may keep them lower than in Western countries.

As noted, any severe financial disruption in Japan would spread to the U.S. The same is true of a depression there. Given the tremendous imbalances in the world, a severe business downturn in the second largest economy would not be self-contained.

10

Eleven Economic Themes
for Equity Investors --
Why Financial Assets, not Tangibles
Remain the Long-Run Winners

The stock market crash of 1987 came as a shock, but it was not entirely unexpected. We pointed out in a report to clients at the end of January 1987 that the stock market explosion had left dull old fundamentals in its wake and was soaring on the wings of speculation. The market was no longer being driven by declining interest rates as it had been from the beginning of the rally in the early 1980s until the end of 1986. Interest rates were stable in early 1987, and increased later in the year even though stock prices continued to soar.

Neither was the rising market pushed by earnings, which had been disappointing to Wall Street analysts and many others for four consecutive years. Normally, securities analysts overestimate corporate earnings when the economy is unexpectedly soft, but underestimate in business expansions when sales growth is strong. Nevertheless, Wall Street analysts collectively overestimated earnings in 1983, 1984, 1985, and 1986 -- all years of business growth.

Furthermore, many forecasters were looking for 20% gains in operating profits in 1987 and 1988. Although this might happen in individual companies, it was highly unlikely that the corporate sector as a whole could enjoy 20% gains in operating earnings for those two years, as we observed in a May 1987 client report. For operating profits to grow that fast in 1987 and 1988, productivity would have to spurt strongly, given the moderate growth in the economy and therefore in corporate sales that we and other forecasters expected. This would curtail employment growth and reduce income gains to the point that real after-tax personal incomes would actually decline in both years. Such a decline has occurred only once in the postwar era -- in 1974, in the midst of a serious recession when the explosion of commodity prices was transferring U.S. purchasing power to OPEC and other commodity producers abroad. Unless saving rates dropped virtually to zero, there probably wouldn't be sufficient sales volume to have any earnings growth at all. A zero saving rate would require so much additional debt by so many consumers as to virtually ensure a collapse in borrowing and spending. Moreover, the saving rate was already at a postwar low, and rates around zero haven't been seen since the 1930s Depression.

Instead of being pushed by fundamentals, we reasoned in early 1987 that stocks were being driven by the belief that vast quantities of money here and abroad had no place to go but into U.S. stocks. Waning interest in tangible assets, rapid growth in money supplies in major countries, the need to invest 1986 IRA money, the reinvestment of funds gained from the stock market sell-off late in 1986 that was induced by the U.S. tax law changes, and the attractiveness of U.S. stocks to foreign investors after the dollar became cheaper -- all gave credence to this theory.

This theory, we said, in January 1987, "has the smell of a self-feeding rationalization for a speculative stock market that seems to be leaving fundamentals far astern. . . . a full-blown speculative market could be developing and could have far to go as more and more American and foreign investors are drawn in. The similarities with the highly speculative but ultimately disastrous stock market of the late 1920s are striking."

As noted in Chapters 6 and 7, the Crash may prove to be the shock that will precipitate consumer retrenchment and lead to a recession -- or even a 1930s-style depression, with a 10%-20% probability. Nevertheless, that still means that we expect an 80%-90% chance of no more than a series of serious recessions, so it does seem reasonable to consider a long-term investment strategy, other than liquidating everything and putting the proceeds under the mattress.

Long-Term Investment Strategy

As discussed above and in The World Has Definitely Changed, four new forces should dominate investment performance over the next decade:

1) The shift from global shortages to surpluses, which implies continuing intense global competition, ongoing cost-cutting responses by American business, and low inflation if not deflation;

2) The shift in American economic driving forces from basic industry and construction to, in time, high-tech industries and services;

3) The polarization in American household incomes; and

4) Protectionism and financial crises, which threaten global financial stability.

Which Investments Are Best?

Given these four new forces, tangible assets will not be very attractive, but bonds and stocks could be very interesting over the next decade.
● Tangible Assets. Low inflation -- if not deflation -- and other factors we see ahead are not very hospitable to the prices of coins, antiques, real estate, and other tangible assets that were such sure winners in the inflationary 1970s.

Of course, money can still be made in real estate and other tangible assets. Quality office buildings that are well located and fully leased to prime tenants are almost always winners. Not every real estate investment fits that category, however. I have a standing joke with a number of our real estate clients that before they close the coffin lid on me, I want to meet someone who owns a lousy building that is poorly located and occupied by crummy tenants. Everybody knows of their existence, but no one I've met admits to owning one. The point is that in the world we foresee, investing in tangibles will no longer be a matter of floating pleasantly with the tide, but rather treading in motionless water or, more likely, swimming vigorously upstream against a stiff current.

● Bonds. We continue to believe that 30-year Treasury bonds may almost double in price as their yields fall from their current 8.5% level to our eventual target of 4%-5%, and that other quality bonds will also do very well. We derive this target for 30-year Treasuries by adding our long-term forecast of 2% inflation to the normal 2%-3% inflation-adjusted, or real, rate of interest. Furthermore, 2% inflation may prove to be on the high side, so yields could fall to even lower levels once investors become convinced, perhaps by a serious recession, that the much-feared inflation of the 1970s is finally over.

● Stocks. Declining interest rates should push up stock price-to-earnings ratios (P/Es). Add to this the 9%-10% annual gains in average corporate operating earnings we foresee over the next decade, and the result is a very attractive environment for many, but not all, stocks. Which stocks will do best -- and worst -- in this atmosphere?

A Thematic Approach

The World Has Definitely Changed examines a number of economic themes, 11 of which form the basis of a thematic approach to long-term equity -- or direct -- investment. Many of these themes suggest attractive investment opportunities, while others point to areas that should be avoided or even considered for short sales.

● 1. Bottom-line growth stocks. Historically, growth stocks have been those of companies with the rapid sales volume growth needed to achieve meaningful gains in earnings in the era of high inflation, which systematically transferred corporate profitability to labor and government. Now, serious inflation is probably over, so this transfer of earnings is unlikely, and corporate restructuring is expected to result in cost control and productivity growth. As a result, corporate earnings should grow at a compound rate of 9%-10% over the next decade, assuming no major financial or economic disruptions.

Some firms will be so effective at cutting costs that

their earnings will make their equities look like growth stocks even though they lack the rapid rises in corporate revenues and consequently don't now sell at growth stock P/Es. These are what we have dubbed bottom-line growth stocks, and investors will profit from them in two ways: from the earnings gains themselves, and from the increase in the P/Es of these companies' stocks as investors in time realize the intensity, consistency, and longevity of their cost-cutting efforts.

We examined 52 U.S. manufacturing industries, and used a number of tests to answer four basic questions:

A) Which industries are facing significant pressure to cut costs?

B) Which industries have sizeable costs that can be cut?

C) Which are serious about the matter as revealed by their results in cutting costs in recent years?

D) Perhaps most important, which will be able to retain in earnings the fruits of restructuring and cost control as opposed to seeing them dissipated by competition?

Obviously, some bottom-line growth stocks may be found in industries that do not look attractive on the basis of our answers to these 4 questions, but among those that do, but we have earmarked for further study inorganic chemicals, rubber, photographic equipment, tobacco, aerospace, engines and turbines, aircraft, iron and steel foundries, drugs, and communications equipment. The complete list of all 52 industries, ranked from most to least likely to contain bottom-line growth stocks is shown in FIGURE 19.

• 2. <u>Deregulation of American industry</u> seems to have slowed recently, but even if it doesn't resume, the cumulative effects of what has taken place so far will provide immense investment opportunities -- and pitfalls -- in the brokerage and investment banking industry, airlines,

FIGURE 19

1. Industrial Inorganic Chemicals
2. Tires & Inner Tubes
3. Photographic Equipment & Supplies
4. Cigarettes
5. Guided Missiles, Space Vehicles, & Parts
6. Engines & Turbines
7. Aircraft & Parts
8. Iron & Steel Foundries
9. Drugs
10. Communications Equipment
11. Electrical Industrial Apparatus
12. Measuring & Controlling Devices
13. Nonferrous Rolling & Drawing
14. Electronic Components & Accessories
15. Household Appliances
16. Newspapers
17. Metalworking Machinery
18. Blast Furnace & Basic Steel Products
19. General Industrial Machinery
20. Motor Vehicles & Equipment
21. Medical Instruments & Supplies
22. Cutlery, Hand Tools, & Hardware
23. Weaving Mills, Cotton
24. Soap, Cleaners, & Toilet Goods
25. Periodicals
26. Electrical Lighting & Wiring Equipment
27. Metal Forgings & Stampings
28. Preserved Fruits & Vegetables
29. Industrial Organic Chemicals
30. Grain Mill Products
31. Knitting Mills
32. Paper Mills, Except Building Paper
33. Misc. Converted Paper Products
34. Plastic Materials & Synthetics
35. Paperboard Containers & Boxes
36. Toys & Sporting Goods
37. Concrete, Gypsum, & Plaster Products
38. Fabricated Structural Metal Products
39. Glass & Glassware, Pressed or Blown
40. Commercial Printing
41. Misc. Plastic Products
42. Household Furniture
43. Sawmills & Planing Mills
44. Construction & Related Machinery
45. Millwork, Plywood, & Structural Members
46. Office & Computing Machines
47. Meat Products
48. Men's & Boys' Furnishings
49. Women's And Misses' Outerwear
50. Footwear, Except Rubber
51. Primary Nonferrous Metals
52. Petroleum Refining

trucks, buses, railroads, telecommunications, financial services, oil and gas, and other deregulated industries.

Timing is particularly important with any investment, but even more important in a deregulated industry. Initially, almost every participant believes it will not only be a survivor, but ultimately a much bigger firm. Consequently, deregulation leads to the invasion of others' territories, counterattacks, and general cutthroat competition until the least efficient and the financially weak are eliminated.

Braniff, now all but gone as an airline, tried to become a coast-to-coast carrier when deregulation permitted unlimited expansion, but ran into a devastating reaction from American Airlines in several key markets.

Eventually, when consolidation takes place and warfare winds down, opportunities for attractive profits' growth will develop. This all takes time, and so far the risks seem to be in being too early, not too late. Airline fare wars keep popping up even after almost ten years of deregulation and the elimination of half a dozen major carriers.

The Crash and the overexpansion and excessive risks taken by a number of Wall Street firms in recent years suggest that another round of consolidation is imminent, even though fixed brokerage commissions were eliminated way back in 1975. Despite the tremendous consolidation that's taken place so far in commercial banking, it's still too early to outline the eventual mix and relative power of small banks, regionals, super-regionals, and the money center banks, especially with serious loan problems in energy, agriculture, real estate, and the international area still unresolved.

• 3. <u>Problems with basic industries</u>, such as steel and autos, will continue unless the U.S. resorts to all-out protectionism. As technology in many basic industries is now universally available, the only fundamental differences among countries are productivity levels and labor and transportation costs. In many cases, U.S. industries still retain cartel-like mentality and cost structures, which retard productivity growth and drive away innovation and capital investment. In the auto industry, Ford and General Motors signed labor contracts in 1987 that severely limit their ability to cut out unneeded production workers.

With the recently weakened dollar and some improvement in labor and management attitudes and cost structures, a number of basic American industries have begun to be competitive with Europe and Japan. At the same time, however, production in these industries is shifting rapidly to the newly industrialized countries that tend to tie their currencies to the dollar, as noted in Chapter 3. Even if they didn't, it wouldn't make much difference. The gap between South Korean steel workers using state-of-the-art equipment and who are paid about $2 an hour and their American counterparts, paid more than ten times as much, seems unlikely to narrow enough to prevent a continuing erosion of that industry, regardless of what currencies do. In the long run, American firms in basic industries that stick to niches and proprietary products may be attractive, but those competing directly with the NICs seem doomed.

● 4. The ongoing polarization of American household incomes, as discussed in Chapter 5, will have immense implications for spending and saving patterns. Retailers like Bloomingdale's and Tiffany's serving the top-income people will continue to benefit, as will those like Walmart that sell to low-income people. But middle-market retailers, like Sears and Penney's, will be squeezed along with their customers.

Upscale recreation, travel, and other services that upper-income people favor will be big winners. In particular, the shift in income and assets to higher-income hands will greatly increase the funds available for investment and the need for financial services, as is already well known. Every major bank that's worth its salt already has a Private Banking Division to serve customers with large assets and big incomes, complete with French provincial desks instead of austere and foreboding tellers' cages.

Nevertheless, we're at least as intrigued by the opportunities to service the formerly middle-income families who are being pushed down because those opportunities are virtually unknown and unexplored. Maybe they'll spend less on luxuries, but buy the very best of the small ones they can afford. Surveys show that lower-income people often drink much higher-priced Scotch than I do. Preserving the middle-class dignity of those who are pushed down income-wise opens other opportunities. A bank that makes them feel like individuals, not numbers, but at service fees they can afford will be a sure winner.

• 5. <u>Low inflation -- or even deflation</u> -- will mean continuing problems for producers of commodities, including oil. Conversely, users of commodities will benefit to the extent that price weakness for materials is not simply passed through to their customers. Industries in which inputs of commodities are relatively small may save less from weak prices of those inputs, but may be better off than many in keeping those savings since they are less conspicuous.

• 6. <u>Interest rate- and inflation-sensitive industries</u> such as utilities, and a number of regional banks, insurance companies, and savings and loans will enjoy the atmosphere we see ahead. Telephone, electric and other utilities, with their need to refinance past borrowing will benefit from the substantial decline in interest rates we expect, as well as any reductions in other costs, including energy. True, non-interest cost savings are ultimately passed through to the users of their services, but the delays in the regulatory process will allow utilities to do so with lags.

Similarly, regional banks benefit from declining interest rates. Many of their loans to smaller businesses and consumers are tied to the prime rate, which tends to lag behind borrowing costs when interest rates fall. Furthermore, declining interest rates increase the returns on banks' portfolios of government bonds. Nevertheless, the structure of bank loan portfolios needs to be considered carefully. Even those that have successfully avoided problems in energy, agriculture, real estate, and foreign loans may have heavy dependence on consumer borrowing through credit cards, installment, and home equity loans. If, as we expect, consumers switch from heavy borrowing to debt repayment, banks without alternative sources of growth could suffer.

Strong savings and loans will benefit as declining interest rates spur mortgage demand. However, weakness in real estate prices and consumer retrenchment could offset much of this benefit. Furthermore, many savings and loans remain in deep financial trouble. There is a risk that a wave of bankruptcies or forced government interventions could panic investors into dumping good ones as well. Like the REITs a decade ago, the cops could take the good girls as well as the bad ones when they arrive.

Property and casualty insurance companies also benefit from lower inflation rates, which hold down the cost of settling claims, and from lower interest rates and higher stock prices, which benefit their investment portfolios. Nevertheless, there is growing evidence that the industry is now at a cyclical underwriting peak, and cuts in premium rates and competition may become very fierce, at least in the next several years.

• 7. <u>Single-family housing</u> is still attractive for about the next five years as the last of the postwar babies buy their first houses, but activity will continue to vary geographically. Like everything else in the oil patch, single-family housing is hopelessly overbuilt. Housing activity in the New York area and other locations that benefited from the tremendous money made in financial services in general and on Wall Street in particular in the last five years may suffer with the ending of the corporate finance boom, as an aftermath of the stock market crash, and from the cost cutting being done by banks and insurance companies. Nevertheless, other areas of the country such as the Southeast and the West Coast remain strong.

Housing and other forms of real estate may be devastated, however, if deflation sets in. For most individuals, the idea of a declining price for their biggest asset, their house, is unthinkable on anything but a short-term basis. Such a decline would only reinforce the effects of the consumer retrenchment and debt repayment that we see ahead, and could precipitate a massive problem with consumer confidence. After all, a house is not only a big but also a highly discretionary purchase that people can postpone if they are cautious and attempting to reliquify.

● 8. Protectionism may not sound like an investment theme. It is certainly true that it invites retaliation and generally reduces world trade and economic activity to the detriment of most industries. Nevertheless, there are some winners from protectionism, at least in the relative sense. Already, the forest products industry has benefited from the U.S. pressure on Canada to increase the cost of Canadian exports of wood products to the U.S. The American semiconductor industry has gained from the ongoing trade dispute with Japan over the dumping of semiconductors.

The stock market crash reminded Congress of the collapse in 1929 and the subsequent contributions of the 1930 Smoot-Hawley tariffs to the Depression that followed. Consequently, protectionist zeal has eased a bit in Washington, but as noted in Chapter 7, the real road test will come during the next recession, when both Congress and consumers will be blaming it on foreigners.

● 9. Financial crises also offer investment opportunities, especially on the short side of the market, for some of the victims of Third World debt defaults, problems for U.S. agriculture, S & L defaults, strained leveraged buyouts, and overbuilt real estate. Conversely, although few publicly held companies are available, those involved in restructuring failed leveraged buyouts, savings & loans, and real estate properties should do very well in the next decade. The business of retraining, counseling, and relocating people whose jobs will be eliminated through cost cutting and restructuring should thrive. In fact, the workout or restructuring business looks like a true growth industry. The only problem is that it needs a sexier name!

● 10. Capital equipment looks like the most rapidly growing segment of the economy in the next decade, with emphasis on equipment that assists business in cutting costs and improving productivity as it strives to meet global competition. We see this component of GNP rising from 8.4% of the total in 1987 to an unprecedented 11.9%

in 1997. Demand from all sorts of equipment will be strong, including electronics, automatic transfer equipment, instruments, and flexible manufacturing equipment.

.• 11. Business services that help cut costs will also benefit from the atmosphere that we see ahead. Temporary employment services should thrive as more people are hired for only the time of day or the season of year that they are needed, as noted above. Also, temporary people are generally lower cost since they receive fewer fringe benefits. Furthermore, the use of outside people and their growing availability reduces the urge to hire people ahead of actual need, which characterized and magnified labor shortages in the past.

Consulting and other services that assist business to cut costs and increase productivity should be in high demand. In this regard, the inputs of clear-eyed, sure-footed, and clairvoyant economic consultants will be indispensable.

Portfolio Strategy for a Recession/Depression

All may be well in the long run, but in the meanwhile, the outlook is for a recession of unknown depth -- it could be anything from mild to a 1930s-style depression. This certainly suggests a cautious investment strategy with emphasis on safety and liquidity until the extent of the next recession is known. It hardly seems like an inflationary era that would favor illiquid real estate and other tangible assets, but how about stocks and bonds?

U.S. Treasury obligations and high-quality municipal bonds should be upstanding investments, both in terms of safety and due to the substantial decline in interest rates we expect. The next recession could reduce inflationary expectations significantly, since it will probably close off the first business expansion since the late 1950s that did not deteriorate into inflation. Many believe that every expansion ends with a burst of inflation, and can't remember back to the 1950s, or still were in grade school at the time. The only way that anyone knows that the business expansion is over is for the next recession to arrive, and if we're right, that recession will confirm that serious inflation is over. Hence, our moniker, <u>the confirming recession</u>.

A serious recession could move yields a considerable distance toward our final target of 4%-5% on 30-year Treasury bonds and spell tremendous appreciation in those and other quality bonds. We particularly like Treasury obligations since they have three sterling qualities -- first, they are the best credits in the world; second, they will not be called away in the event that interest rates plummet and their prices soar; and third, they are among the most liquid of instruments so they can be bought and sold in high quantities without disturbing the market. As we've discussed in the past, however, junk and other low-quality bonds would deteriorate in an environment of recession or worse as they did in the wake of the stock market crash.

Investment-grade bonds that are less than top-quality may have small risks of default, but the yields they currently provide over and above the Treasury rates seem inadequate, given the prospects for a deep recession or worse, and its effect on corporate earnings. Ironically, top-grade corporate bonds are also risky, not because of possible defaults, but due to the possibility that the issuing companies will be the subjects of leverage buyouts financed by huge quantities of junk bonds. As many sad cases already testify, the result is likely to be the downgrading of the bond ratings of outstanding issues and the resulting fall in their prices. A near-term recession makes lower bond yields seem almost inevitable. In fact, we find a lot of merit in the BBB bond strategy suggested to us by a good friend and client of ours on the West Coast. This doesn't mean buying lower-quality bonds, those of bbb credit ratings. In fact, the best quality bonds are none too good. Rather, BBB stands for Buy Bonds Blindly. We only hope that we don't have to shift to another BBB bond strategy soon and well before our targets are met -- Bail out of Bonds Boldly!

There are three caveats to the BBB bond strategy. First, if excessive Federal Reserve ease or a collapse in the dollar convinces financial markets that serious inflation is imminent, interest rates could skyrocket. This would, however, only increase the odds of a serious recession which would so weaken the economy here and abroad as to kill all inflationary fears and lead to much lower interest rates.

Second, a collapse in the dollar might convince the Fed that it needed to raise interest rates to attract funds back to the U.S. This would be similar to its 1931 increase in the discount rate, instituted to ward off fears that the U.S. was abandoning the gold standard. The U.K. had gone off the gold standard, and foreign banks, fearing that the U.S. would follow, were withdrawing their deposits from American banks. As a result, Treasury bond yields rose to levels that actually exceeded the 1929 peak, and the prices of low quality bonds collapsed as confidence in the viability of their issuers evaporated. Like the 1931 action, any Fed-led increase in interest rates this time would only insure a recession or worse, which would then result in substantially lower interest rates.

Third, as noted in Chapter 9, the collapse in the highly speculative Japanese stock market could push down U.S. bond prices as Japanese investors sold their U.S. holdings in order to support their own stock market. They probably would not be successful in staving off considerable financial strains, and the Japanese recession that would follow, coupled with a U.S. business downturn, would almost guarantee a global business slump or worse. In this environment, U.S. Treasury bonds and other quality fixed-income instruments would look like safe havens, especially if a full-blown depression developed in Japan. Rebounds in both the dollar and quality U.S. bonds would only be a matter of time.

11

Twelve Critical Elements
of a Business Strategy
for a Changed World
Facing a Recession of Unknown Depth

In a changed world that's facing a recession of unknown depth, a much different business strategy is needed than was appropriate from the end of World War II through the 1970s, when strong demand and shortages dominated the business climate. We have identified 12 elements in this new strategy that managers may find useful:

• 1. <u>Accept the reality of fierce ongoing competition.</u> Despite the current concerns about shortages and tight capacity, we're in a world of surpluses for the long haul. This means excruciating ongoing competition. Waiting in the hope that the good old days of shortages will return on a long-term basis may prove disastrous.

• 2. <u>Educate management and labor about the new reality.</u> Management attitudes must be changed permanently, not just temporarily by another layer of directives. A good bureaucrat stuck in the old ways can beat the best intentions of senior management any day. Labor may need examples, such as taking representative groups from the factory floor to Taiwan to see how hard the competition works and how little they get paid for their efforts. When they get back, the word will spread to their peers.

• 3. <u>Be consistent and set good examples.</u> General Motors is not alone, but it certainly has had its share of problems in this area. Not too long ago, the auto giant ended cost-of-living escalators for white-collar workers and replaced them with merit pay raises only. This was certainly a good idea and long overdue, but shortly thereafter the firm announced a 20% stock buyback program. Morale fell as employees felt as if they were being squeezed to bail out stockholders. Earlier, right before a new United Auto Workers' contract negotiation, GM paid some sizable management bonuses. Roger Smith, the chairman, was undoubtedly entitled to a million-dollar bonus, but the example it set going into the wage negotiations was most unfortunate.

● 4. <u>Be cautious until the next recession comes and goes.</u> As noted, it may be a normal recession, but then again it could touch off protectionist pressures and financial crises that could turn it into something much more severe, even a 1930s-style depression. It makes a great deal of sense to have a lot of dry powder until the full extent of that recession is known.

● 5. <u>Control costs.</u> In a world of surpluses with fierce competition, most firms will be unable to pass on costs through price increases, so they must control them to remain in business, and cut them even further for attractive profits growth. It's important for both management and labor to realize that they're all in it together, and that maintaining a strong organization by controlling costs is the best way to protect everyone's job.

A zero-based management organization approach is helpful. The idea is to start with the minimum number of people it takes to run the organization, and then build the organization chart around it, not the other way around. Eliminating people but leaving their positions on the chart makes it tempting to fill those empty boxes. Eliminating minor and unprofitable lines of business is another way to cut costs permanently, as is reducing the number of suppliers. Being able to reward suppliers who meet quality standards with bigger orders tends to result in lower bids.

Labor costs can be attacked by moving operations to lower-cost areas in the U.S. or abroad, and by using "voluntary" early retirees who return as consultants doing the same job at less pay and with few fringe benefits.

Two-tier wage systems, in which new employees get 40% or 50% less for doing the same jobs, is another approach to the problem, as is employing part-time workers who have fewer fringes and who are employed only at the time of day or season they're needed.

Materials costs are also important, and can be controlled more than many realize. Far too often the head of purchasing is a low-level employee reporting to a plant manager, even though purchased materials may be the largest cost element for the company. The purchasing head should be a well-qualified individual reporting to senior management. Furthermore, better cost control results may be had if purchasing managers are engineers who have run plants and have a clear understanding of specifications and acceptable substitutes.

• 6. Stick to businesses you know and manage for long-run results. This is an era of conglomerate busting, the recent wave of leveraged buyouts and takeovers notwithstanding. Given the ongoing pressure to cut costs and the inability to pass them on through price increases, it's a time when understanding the business on the factory floor or in the office is more important than manipulating a financial portfolio of companies. Furthermore, in the grueling global competitive battle, long-term performance, not short-term profits, should be emphasized. Short-term performance often comes by milking assets at the expense of the investment and innovation that pay off big only in the long run.

• 7. Share company risks with suppliers and employees. Suppliers and employees have been accustomed to ongoing increases in prices and wages whether or not their costs were increasing in inflation-adjusted terms. It's a cultural shock to face the idea of nearly static prices and wages. Nevertheless, that is a necessity in the world of low inflation or deflation we see ahead. Furthermore, in the past, if a group of employees were paid too much, or business conditions changed such that they were no longer economically effective, high inflation worked in a company's favor. It was only a matter of holding back pay increases for those employees and waiting for inflation to wipe out the excess. Now, however, inflation will no longer be there to wash away a company's mistakes.

Exxon ran into this situation in 1986. A merit pay system had elevated the pay of a number of middle-management people to levels that may have been acceptable when oil was selling for over $30 a barrel but were simply uneconomic at oil prices of $15 a barrel. Without escalating oil prices, time was not on Exxon's side in correcting this problem, so the company carried out draconian cuts of 25% of its middle-management work force -- 50% at some headquarters' operations. Moreover, the company encouraged older people to retire and replaced them with younger, less costly people. True, the younger workers were not always as productive, but they were lower-cost to the point that they more than made up for their lack of experience.

The effects of this sort of catharsis on morale are extreme, so it makes more sense to share the risks with employees and suppliers such that if business conditions change, there's an automatic adjustment process, rather than the need for traumatic layoffs or changes in supplier relationships.

In the case of suppliers, it may make sense for a firm to take equity positions in them. This will let them know that there is a long-term relationship, and give them an incentive to invest to meet quality specifications, tight delivery schedules, and other stringent customer requirements. In other words, they will know they're on the same team, and overall productivity will be enhanced.

Pay more from the bottom line

In the case of employees, meaningful amounts of compensation should be linked to company or divisional performance. This can take the form of productivity sharing, pay for knowledge, profit-sharing, stock option plans, etc. A number of favorable results can be expected. First, it creates incentives for everyone to be much more productive. Secondly, it automatically corrects for problems and changes in the company's fortunes.

Sure, nobody likes to take pay cuts, but in the world we see ahead, whenever business turns down without the cushion of inflation, pay cuts may well be necessary. Paying people substantial amounts from the bottom line means that those pay cuts are effective immediately, with the arguing done later and not while the company is still paying oversized amounts. This avoids the problem U.S.X. had a while back, when the company fought many years with the United Steel Workers over pay concessions, suffered a six-month strike, and still got few results.

More compensation linked to company results will probably also be needed for middle as well as upper management in the world we see ahead. The need for cost control and restructuring is bringing about departures of people on all levels and at every size of company, and the safety of employment in large corporations no longer exists. Earlier, many traded off the opportunities for higher rewards but higher risks at smaller companies for the security and certainty of jobs at large corporations. With this no longer possible, incentives for valued managers at all levels are needed at larger corporations to offset the increased risks.

In some cases, it's easier to share the risks with employees in the fringe area than it is with cash compensation. In a number of companies, medical coinsurance used to be common but was subsequently replaced by plans paid for entirely by the company. Now, coinsurance is returning and it not only reduces costs for medical procedures, but also cuts out what we call "recreational medicine" -- when an employee feels any ache or pain, he doesn't hesitate to take the afternoon off to see a physician, since he's not paying any part of the cost. Other companies are shifting from defined benefit pension plans, in which the company is responsible for pension payments irrespective of the investment success of the funds set aside, to defined contribution plans in which the employee shares the investment risk on the funds contributed on his behalf by the company.

• 8. Emphasize volume expansion. With the likely end of inflation or even deflation making cost pass-through difficult, and global competition putting unit profitability under continuing pressure, volume expansion will be very important in promoting overall growth in a firm's earnings.

Chapters 10 and 12 discuss a number of industries and business sectors that should achieve attractive growth in the years ahead, and also list some that look like under-performers and therefore should be avoided or abandoned. Furthermore, the next three business strategy elements discussed before may be helpful in achieving attractive volume and profitability growth in a wide variety of businesses.

• 9. <u>In commodity businesses, be the low-cost producer or get out.</u> Commodity businesses are those in which the technology is universally available, and the product is indistinguishable. In a world of surpluses, the key to success is being the low-cost producer, and the cost differences often boil down to essentially those of labor and transportation since raw materials and other costs are similar for all producers, as noted in Chapter 10. In such industries with excess capacity and strong competition, having the second lowest cost doesn't count. To achieve the status of low-cost producer it may be necessary to move production to a lower-cost area in the U.S. or to move it abroad. If a firm can't become the low-cost producer, it should seriously consider exiting the business, unless other considerations, such as the need to produce a complete product line, prevail.

• 10. <u>Explore niche businesses.</u> These can be safe havens from the nonstop onslaught of foreign competition in basic commodity-producing industries. Niches can include special sizes and shapes, businesses where high service content or fast delivery time is important, or areas where fad or fashion change so fast that it would be impossible to get the items made in Hong Kong and shipped to the U.S. before demand for them disappears.

• 11. <u>Develop proprietary products.</u> This, too, is a safe haven from relentless global competition. Even commodities can be turned into proprietary products with additional elements, particularly add-on services.

A friend of ours manufactures stationery in Minneapolis. The quality is superb, and the watermarks are beautiful. Still, writing paper and envelopes are commodities, only requiring the purchase of good quality paper and the machinery to cut and fold it and apply the glue to the envelopes. This firm, however, has created proprietary products through unusual levels of services and very effective marketing. For example, before a salesman makes a cold call on a prospect, someone goes to the library and researches where that person grew up, went to school, his hobbies, clubs, interests, who he married, what his children do, etc. Then when the salesman walks through the door, he can greet the prospect like a long-lost friend. Obviously, this enhances the odds of a sale of something that would otherwise only be a commodity.

• 12. <u>Build financial strength.</u> In a world of rapid change, long-term surpluses and a recession of unknown depth out there somewhere, financial strength is imperative. It is the ammunition with which to fight the ongoing wars for survival and success. Financial strength means building a fortress-like balance sheet. It means resisting the urge to buy companies that are bargains -- there may be bigger bargains later -- or the urge to buy back the company's stock because it's cheap -- it may be even cheaper later.

Financial strength also means cultivating relationships with potential sources of funds, keeping them abreast of the company's results and plans, so that when their resources are needed, there is an ongoing understanding as to why and a willingness to provide them. Meeting a lending officer of the firm's bank for the first time during a company financial crisis is hardly the sensible approach.

12

Long-Run Winners Are
Capital Equipment and
the Trade Sector,
While the Losers Are
Consumer and Government Spending

Our forecast for the economy and its major components for the next decade assumes that the next recession does not turn into a 1930s-type depression which would dominate the next decade; the absence of crises elsewhere in the world that could severely affect the U.S.; no dramatic arms accord with the Soviets; and no severe supplier disruptions in oil or other key commodities.

A New Approach to Tax Policy

We also assume no dramatic changes in the federal tax structure. A value-added tax may be considered seriously in coming years, but we believe that voters will insist on maintaining the essence of the Tax Reform Act of 1986 with its lower tax rates and other reforms. Everyone wants a lower deficit, but few volunteer to have their taxes increased or, for that matter, ask for their benefits from government spending to be cut. Many complain about a lack of leadership in Washington on the deficit problem, but voters aren't providing much followership.

The reforms of the 1986 tax act are profound and will definitely encourage greater efficiency in the American economy. The tax system's purpose, of course, has always been to raise revenues, but in the past 50 years it has also been increasingly used to achieve specific economic and social goals advocated by the various Administrations and Congresses. For example, the tax system has been used to promote low-income housing, consumer borrowing, and office building construction, and the lower tax rate on capital gains favored long-term holdings of investments.

The new approach, in contrast, is to remove the specific incentives and tax shelters, reduce corporate and individual income tax rates, and let the free market direct business, personal spending, and investment decisions. Perhaps most important, for most purposes it removes the distinction between income and capital gains by equalizing the tax rates on the two.

Free markets allocate resources more efficiently than Washington, so the new law will improve the efficiency of the economy. Furthermore, it will redeploy some of the nation's finest minds that earlier concentrated on tax law and accounting, and on developing and marketing tax shelters that converted income into capital gains, to productive work. This does not suggest that these people were useless. Indeed, we all had the privilege, almost the necessity, of relying on their talents to minimize tax burdens. But in terms of helping the nation compete in an increasingly competitive world, they have been of no value -- or even of negative value since they facilitated the divergence of our attention away from productive work and investment, and toward beating taxes.

Losers and Winners

We look for real gross national product growth of about 3% per year over the next decade, which is stronger than in the previous 15 years, but weaker than in the catch-up decades of the 1950s and 1960s. This average allows for several serious recessions over the next decade, but not a full blown Kondratieff Wave depression or a rerun of the 1930s.

As shown in FIGURE 20, consumer spending should decline from 65.3% of GNP in 1987 to 60.5% in 1997, a substantial retrenchment, which will bring consumer outlays back to its share level in 1969. This results from two causes. First the ongoing squeeze on costs should keep real disposable, or after-tax, income growing slightly slower than GNP. Secondly, the rise in the saving rate we discussed earlier means that consumer spending will grow more slowly than disposable income.

The government is also expected to be a loser at the

FIGURE 20

	1972A	1979A	1987P	1992E	1997E
Gross National Product	100.0%	100.0%	100.0%	100.0%	100.0%
Consumption	62.2	62.8	65.3	63.5	60.5
Durables	7.7	8.3	10.2	9.2	9.3
Nondurables	25.5	24.0	22.9	22.0	20.8
Services	29.0	30.4	32.2	32.2	30.5
Nonres. Fixed Investment	10.6	12.2	11.7	12.9	15.3
Structures	4.2	4.1	3.3	3.2	3.5
Prod. Durable Equipment	6.4	8.1	8.4	9.7	11.9
Inventory Investment	0.8	0.5	1.1	0.0	0.7
Residential Construction	6.4	5.4	5.1	5.3	5.4
Total Government	21.9	19.1	20.2	20.8	19.5
Federal	9.4	7.4	8.8	8.9	8.0
Defense	7.1	5.1	6.9	6.8	6.0
Nondefense	2.3	2.3	1.9	2.1	2.0
State & Local	12.4	11.7	11.4	11.9	11.5
Net Exports	-1.9	0.1	-3.5	-2.4	-1.5
Exports	7.5	11.2	11.1	11.9	12.2
Imports	9.4	11.1	14.7	14.3	13.7

SOURCE: U.S. Dept. of Commerce

federal level, where we see government purchases of goods and services declining from 8.8% of GNP in 1987 to 8.0% in 1997. This is a result of the continuing budget deficit and voter pressure to hold down government spending growth. Assuming that revenues continue to grow in step with the economy -- that no big new tax cuts are enacted -- this will allow a gradual decrease in the deficit to the point that it will be largely eliminated by the mid-1990s. A dramatic arms accord with the U.S.S.R. could shrink defense spending's share of GNP, and hence the deficit much faster, but otherwise, deficit elimination will be a slow process.

Residential construction's will be just about static. In 1987 it contributed 5.1% of GNP, and we see about the same number in 1997. Nonresidential investment in structures' share also will be fairly level, remaining weak in the near term, until excess hotels, shopping centers, and office buildings are absorbed. After that, when new construction again gets under way, we expect that sector to contribute about 3.5% of GNP.

The most dramatic winner we foresee is producers' durable equipment. This will play a key role in the cost control and productivity improvement needed to make U.S. industry once again competitive on an international scale. As noted in Chapter 10, we see the sector moving from 8.4% of GNP in 1987 to 11.9% in 1997, a level that is unprecedented in the postwar period.

We also see gradual improvement in the U.S. trade balance, although the deficit will still be meaningful in 10 years. Exports of goods and services are expected to grow at a 4.7% annual rate over the next decade. Although this is almost twice the 2.7% expected growth in imports, imports are so much bigger than exports that the overall net export deficit will only slowly be reduced from 3.5% of GNP in 1986 (in National Income and Product Account terms), to 1.5% in 1997.

Index of Recent Shilling & Co.
Research Reports
Used in Preparing This Book

Japanese Cost Control: Can It Offset the Strong Yen?
(January 26, 1987)

Overcoming adversity often leads to strength, and Japan's intense cost control efforts in the face of the strong yen -- which surpass anything seen in the U.S. in the early 1980s, when the dollar was strong -- suggest that Japanese firms may soon emerge as even more formidable competitors.

Stocks vs. Bonds -- The Great Divergence
(January 31, 1987)

The bull stock market in the last four and a half years has been driven by declining interest rates, but now stocks are leaving fundamentals far behind. This suggests extreme caution in investment strategy as similarities with the late 1920s become stark.

Bottom-Line Growth Stocks (February 25, 1987)

An exciting new investment concept is developing in this era of cost control: bottom-line growth stocks. These are the equities of companies that are so successful in cutting costs that their bottom-line earnings will skyrocket, even though they may lack the volume growth associated with the traditional growth stock category. Stockholders should benefit from both earnings growth and higher price-to-earnings ratios as the markets appreciate these changes.

Oil Prices -- Can OPEC Hold Them Up? (March 12, 1987)
    The Saudis are once again acting as swing producers,
    which probably foreshadows a repeat performance of
    last year's scenario, when oil prices tumbled.

The Weak Dollar -- Is It Inflationary or Deflationary?
(April 21, 1987)
    An eventual improvement in the trade balance due to
    a weaker dollar will come at the expense of other
    countries. Financially weak countries such as those in
    Latin America could easily be thrown into financial
    crises that might precipitate global deflation.

Is 1929 Looming for the U.S. or for Japan?
(April 26, 1987)
    Despite the similarities between the U.S. economy
    today and just prior to the 1930s Depression, a depres-
    sion is more likely in Japan than in the U.S. The
    Japanese stock market is extremely speculative, much
    as was the U.S. market in the late 1920s. More im-
    portant, Japan may experience some difficult transi-
    tions for its economy, much as the U.S. did in the
    1930s, since the bases of its spectacular postwar
    growth have faded.

Home Equity Loans -- Disinheriting the Next Generation
(May 26, 1987)
    The interest payment deductibility changes in the new
    tax law leave home equity loans as the preferred
    source of consumer borrowing. Unless saved by
    another round of serious inflation, Americans, by
    liquidating the remaining equity in their houses, won't
    have it to pass on to their children, who in turn won't
    be able to afford to buy the houses they grew up in.

Would Rapid Earnings Growth in 1987 and 1988 Precipitate a Recession? (May 29, 1987)

If operating profits were 20% in each of the next two years, as many analysts who support the roaring stock market predit, real disposable incomes would likely decline, implying a recession which in turn would devastate the corporate earnings outlook and certainly prevent anything like a 20% increase in profits.

What Hath Citibank Wrought? (June 30, 1987)

Citicorp has boosted its reserves by $3 billion, to protect itself against defaults on its developing country loans. This action, which will probably prove inadequate, may push creditors and debtors further apart, actually enhancing the risk of default. Furthermore, the action has underscored the difference between sound regional banks and weak money center banks.

The Japanese Stock Market -- Opportunities in Weakness? (July 22, 1987)

Although the Japanese stock market is highly vulnerable, it could still soar before a final plunge. A synthetic put can be developed to take advantage of this situation.

Economic Growth -- A Shift of Emphasis, but No Basic Change (August 12, 1987)

As consumer spending has moderated, the source of U.S. economic growth has shifted to the foreign trade sector, although it is uncertain whether the rate of improvement in the trade balance can continue. Furthermore, corporate cost control continues to squeeze consumer incomes, and the borrowing people are doing to maintain the good life is unsustainable. An outside shock will probably cause an agonizing reappraisal and a consumer-led recession. The odds of it starting before the end of 1988 are three to one.

Oh, No! Not a Return to Shortages and Inflation!
(August 26, 1987)

World surplus will continue and deflation, not inflation, is still a threat. As import growth has slowed
and export growth accelerated, the action has shifted
to manufacturing, where productivity growth is high.
Furthermore, labor surplus remains ample and wage
restraint continues due to the end of management
paternalism and labor concern over job security, not
wage increases.

What's Bugging Bonds? (August 27, 1987)

The weak bond market has been blamed on expectations of economic overheating, surging inflation,
further dollar weakness, a deteriorating trade balance,
and skyrocketing oil prices. With our forecast of
moderate growth, low inflation, and a stable dollar,
quality bonds are extremely attractive at current
yields.

The End of the American Dream (September 17, 1987)

Global competition has forced American business to
cut costs vigorously for the first time since the Great
Depression. The result is a tremendous squeeze on
middle-income purchasing power, the end of the
American dream of ever-increasing purchasing power
for those pushed to lower-income status. A consumer-
led recession is likely when an outside shock forces
people to face reality.

The Discount Rate Increase -- A Tiger by the Tail?
(September 21, 1987)

The discount rate increase by the Federal Reserve
may not calm jittery financial markets, and could
enhance the odds of a 1988 recession.

The Long-Term Determinants of Investment Strategy
(September 28, 1987)

Four new forces may prove to be preeminent in directing longer-run investment strategy: the shift from global shortages to surpluses; the replacement of high-tech industries and services for basic industries and construction as the U.S. economy's driving forces; income polarization; and the transition problems of protectionism and financial crises.

The Likelihood of a 1988 Recession Just Went Up
(October 28, 1987)

The collapse in the stock market will probably be the shock that we've been expecting to scare consumers into a recession-inducing decline in their borrowing and spending.

After the Crash, What Do You Do? (October 30, 1987)

Faced with a recession of unknown depth -- anything from mild to a 1930s-style depression -- the prudent investor should concentrate on high-quality bonds and "stocks that look like bonds" -- those with secure earnings and sensitivity to declining interest rates.

Are the Markets Now Forecasting Deflation?
(November 10, 1987)

Commodity price declines in the face of a weak dollar are sending deflation messages -- collapse in strong-currency terms.

Long-Term Investment Strategy (November 29, 1987)

The shift from global shortages to surpluses; high-tech industries and services replacing basic industries and construction as the major sources of U.S. business growth; income polarization; and protectionism and financial crises will dominate the investment scene over the next decade. Tangible assets will be very attractive, but bonds and stocks should thrive, barring financial and economic calamity.

Can Government Action Counter a Recession?
(December 2, 1987)

With the size of the economy today, an average post-war recession will increase the federal deficit by over $100 billion, even without any tax cuts or increases in real spending. This would push the already-huge deficit close to $300 billion and deter anti-recessionary fiscal stimuli.

Stalking the Bottom-Line Growth Stock
(December 11, 1987)

Manufacturing industries were examined in our search for bottom-line growth stocks. Those earmarked for further study include: Industrial Inorganic Chemicals; Tires & Inner Tubes; Photographic Equipment & Supplies; Cigarettes; Guided Missiles, Space Vehicles, & Parts; Engines & Turbines; Aircraft & Parts; Iron & Steel Foundries; Drugs; and Communications Equipment.

The Key Financial Event of 1987 Was Not the Stock Market Crash (December 22, 1987)

Rather, it was the loss of control of U.S. financial markets to foreigners, and the lack of easy policy options to regain it, either through dollar manipulation or monetary or fiscal policy changes.

A Boom in Net Exports: An Offset to a Weak U.S. Consumer, but Lethal to Europe and Japan
(January 11, 1988)

If the American consumer shows any appreciable degree of weakness, the reduction of the foreign deficit needed to offset it and avoid a U.S. recession would push Europe and Japan to the brink, if not into recession.

Appendix

I

FEW FEEL MARKET'S "WEALTH EFFECT"

(Los Angeles Times, February 3, 1987.) With the stock market having a spectacular 1987 so far, the "wealth effect" theory has surfaced anew. Some analysts hope that the great personal wealth created by the financial market's mega-rally in the past few years, along with the sense of well-being that it has generated, will encourage financial asset holders to go on a shopping spree.

No one argues that a boost in consumption is sorely needed: The consumer, who in recent quarters has been carrying the economy, is deeply in debt and seems near exhaustion. But whether this new wealth will be spent is another question.

Institutions such as pension funds hold the bulk of financial assets, and of the assets owned by individuals, stocks and bonds are among the most narrowly held. Only one in five households directly owns any stocks or mutual fund shares, and only one in 12 has any bonds or other credit market instruments. Lately, with the markets booming, many small investors have been drawn to stocks and bonds, especially through mutual funds, but those who have meaningful sums invested in such assets still are few. More important, they tend to already be wealthy. Among stock owners, those in the over-$48,000 income bracket held, on average, about $56,000 in stock and mutual funds in 1984, compared to $16,000 for stock investors in the $24,000-$48,000 brackets.

Thus, as financial assets appreciate, the gains accrue mostly to high-income families, who are the least likely to spend them. The roughly 10% of U.S. families in the $48,000-plus group aren't big spenders: they save about 28% of their incomes. And marginal savings rates -- the portion of each additional dollar of income that is saved -- are probably approaching 100% for the wealthier households.

Moreover, recent surveys indicate that heavy spending from capital gains by these high-income households is even less likely now. Among stockholders over 45 -- those old enough to remember severe bear markets of the past -- confidence in the health of the economy has been on the wane for several months. True, young investors are still optimistic, and their enthusiasm has contributed to consumption growth in recent quarters. But older investors tend to be richer, and their bearishness will probably outweigh the optimism of the younger set.

Optimism Could Fade

Plus, what optimism there is may be reversed quickly if a stock market correction occurs, or even if the recent volatility persists. During their ongoing consumption binge, many investors in the under-45 age group have been piling up debt, confident that appreciation of their financial assets will outpace growth of their liabilities. Now, they may see their paper gains evaporate overnight or experience wide swings, while debts remain unchanged.

Many among the shrewder investors also worry about the underlying value of their assets -- and with good cause. Stock prices have risen largely as a result of higher price-to-earnings ratios, which increase as interest rates fall and a lower discounting rate is applied to the stream of future earnings. Earnings themselves, however, have been disappointing. In addition, with the end of inflation and the collapse in tangible asset prices, the value of the assets that produced those earnings has been flat or declining every year since 1980.

More important from the consumer standpoint is that

while financial assets are gaining, the value of more commonly held assets is dwindling. Private homes, for instance, are the cornerstone of most Americans' net worth, with more than 64% of consumers holding equity in their homes. However, the inflation-adjusted value of housing nationally has barely risen since 1978 while mortgage debt has continued to soar, resulting in a 13% decline in home equity between its 1981 peak and 1985. My firm estimates that the double-digit rise in mortgage debt in 1986 further reduced home-equity, probably to around 54% of home value. This is sharply lower than the 64% level of just five years ago, and only a notch above the all-time low of 53% reached in 1966. Since the new tax law makes borrowing against the home the preferred form of raising funds, this record is certain to be broken this year and sometime soon we will enter uncharted territory.

Drop in Equity Holdings

The same is happening with consumers' other assets. Even though the prices of such items as cars, furniture and jewelry have continued to rise, the rapidly rising non-mortgage debt has sapped their net value, and such actual equity holdings have dropped by almost 15% since the 1980 peak.

The dramatic erosion of these very broadly held forms of wealth is indicative of the declining net worth of low- and moderate-income households. Excluding the increase in the value of stocks, bonds and pension funds, consumers' net worth fell 2.5% in 1985, the latest year for which data are available, and likely declined further in 1986, despite the expanding company.

Even as the stock market booms, implying a rise in the value of American companies, the value of non-corporate equity -- proprietorships and partnerships -- is slipping badly. Interestingly, the steepest decline occurred not in the recessionary of 1982, as would be expected, but in 1985.

In part, this reflects the crisis in U.S. agriculture -- farmers lost nearly half the value of their businesses between 1979 and 1985 -- but non-farm partnerships and proprietary businesses also fared badly. And the situation almost certainly worsened in 1986, when the farm crisis deepened and collapsing oil, office space and other real estate prices lowered the value of many limited partnerships. The fact that many older, wealthier investors are also participants in real estate- and oil-based tax shelters may account for their pessimism. They see profits come into one hand and out the other.

In all, real private tangible net worth in the United States fell 0.8% in 1985, a decline exceeded but once in the post-World War II period, in 1982, amid a severe recession. Since financial assets ultimately represent claims on tangible assets, this measure, in effect, gauges the basic buying power of Americans. And last year's lackluster performance of real GNP and the decline in net savings as a percent of GNP make it likely that in 1986 physical wealth posted a second consecutive annual decline.

The effect of the financial market boom mirrors developments on the personal income side. The lucky few, concentrated in the upper-income brackets, are pulling away, while the average wage earner is being squeezed by cost control The decline in total private net worth is probably a sign that consumers are trying to hold onto lifestyles they can no longer afford by borrowing and drawing down their assets.

However, once they realize that the shortfall in incomes is permanent and not a temporary aberration, many consumers will curb their expenditures. Since those whose net worth is increasing -- the affluent households -- are unlikely to make up for this shortfall, the consequences for the consumer-driven U.S. economy may be very serious.

II

SAUDIS LOSING GRIP ON OIL PRICES

(Los Angeles Times, March 31, 1987.) Two months ago, everything seemed to be going right for OPEC. Demand for oil, besides being at its seasonal peak, was strengthened by exceptionally cold weather in Europe. For 1986 as a whole, oil demand rose 2.5% among industrial nations and 3% in the United States, while U.S. production of crude declined 3%. The Aramco partners -- Exxon, Mobil, Chevron and Texaco -- had just agreed to buy Saudi oil at $18 per barrel, ending the "netback" system under which the price of oil was linked to the prices of the refined products. Finally, Saudi Arabia was resuming its role as a "swing producer," adjusting its oil exports to balance supply with demand. To the extent that it could carry out this role, oil prices could be set at any desired level.

In this environment, oil prices should have easily surpassed $20 per barrel and headed to $30; instead, they rose only to $18.50 on the futures market -- the first clue that the Organization of Petroleum Exporting Countries was in trouble. It's now clear that the cartel faces a number of problems.

- The 2.5% growth in industrial nations' oil consumption in 1986 was largely the result of an inventory buildup that occurred when oil prices collapsed. In contrast, the International Energy Agency forecasts a meager 1% growth in demand for 1987.

- The rates for chartered oil tankers have fallen sharply in recent months, a modest pickup in early March notwithstanding. Lots of oil is already being stored in oil tankers around the globe, forming, in effect, a huge floating pipeline.

- Inventories of petroleum products in the United States are running nearly 20 million barrels above last year's levels. Gasoline and fuel oil supplies are, respectively, 5% and 7% higher than a year ago.

- Many refiners are refusing to sign long-term purchase contracts at $18 per barrel because they expect prices to fall. Instead, they are relying on their inventories to cover their current needs. Normally, worldwide primary stocks are drawn down by, at most, 2 million barrels a day in the first quarter of the year; this year, however, the drawdown rate may have reached 3.5 million barrels a day. Secondary stockpiles may be falling by about 500,000 barrels a day.

Meanwhile, petroleum products continue to pour out of refineries. The American Petroleum Institute reported that U.S. refinery utilization in late February stood at 80.1% of capacity, compared to 78.7% last year. Yet there has been no net increase in demand for gasoline in this country, compared to last year. Many refiners are losing money and have cut the price they are willing to pay for crude.

Some OPEC members have, in effect, become involuntary swing producers. The official price of Qatar's oil, for example, is so high that it is unable to sell more than a fraction of its assigned quota.

Financially weak members, on the other hand, are consistently exceeding their quotas in violation of last December's pact. Nigeria is allegedly offering big discounts in order to maintain export volume. There is evidence that Venezuela and Libya are doing the same, and even Saudi Arabia and Kuwait reportedly have sold refined products at market prices that are far below those needed to justify $18-a barrel crude.

Renewed cheating among OPEC members was to be expected. The new accord is simply a return to the strategy that failed so miserably in 1986. The Saudis, by agreeing to balance worldwide supply and demand, have sent a clear message to other producers: Open the oil valves full blast! Already, they have cut their output from their quota of 4.1 million barrels a day to about 2.5 million, and they are determined to reduce their output enough to sop up excess supplies and ride out the storm. They are fully aware that the stakes in this game are high and that if they fail a second time to maintain the prices -- and hence their credibility as a swing producer -- they may not get a third chance.

Meanwhile, oil companies and refineries are unconvinced that prices can be held at $18-a-barrel levels. They are holding out for better deals, which their excess inventories of crude and refined products allow them to do. This suggests that OPEC's output, even though it has fallen an estimated 1.8 million barrels a day from the 15.8-million-barrel ceiling set in December, is too high and may be softening the market further. However, even if in the short run OPEC is able to push oil prices up, the fundamental reality that it faces is not about to change.

After the second oil shock of 1979, oil prices rose so high that demand for oil fell and remained weak even when the world entered a business recovery in 1983. As expected, high oil prices encouraged conservation, promoted a switch to alternative energy sources and stimulated exploration of new or previously uneconomical deposits. The Saudis had to keep reducing their output to accommodate not only the cheaters within OPEC but also new production constantly coming on line. Their output fell to 2 million barrels a day from 10 million, and it was only a matter of time until their patience ran out.

If the current attempt to set a firm $18-a-barrel price fails, it will show that the cartel is no longer effective, and its financially weak members may rush to raise their output. They must maintain their foreign exchange earnings to service their debts, so once the price of their leading export commodity falls, they try to make up the lost revenue on higher volume.

If OPEC loses credibility, how low could oil prices fall? Possibly down to the cost of pumping oil in the Middle East, estimated anywhere from 50 cents to $3 a barrel. There's a lot of hot air between those numbers and current prices, but even this is not necessarily the floor. As we've seen in the case of copper, when a country needs foreign exchange to make debt payments, it will continue to sell its export commodity even if world prices fall below production costs.

The outcome of the tug of war between the Saudis on one side, and cheaters in their own camp and oil consumers who are holding out for lower prices on the other, will be known soon. This is the inventory-reduction time of the year, when excess production is the most damaging. Who will win is far from certain, but the Saudis may well emerge as losers, which could lead to another oil price collapse. If so, it will be one more manifestation of the world of low inflation.

III

JAPAN'S ECONOMY MIMICKING U.S.

(<u>Los Angeles Times</u>, May 23, 1987.) Today's economic conditions are very similar to those of the late 1920's that ushered in the Great Depression.

Then, just as now, pervasive surpluses spurred fierce international competition, with many countries resorting to protectionism. International debt problems emerged, and weak prices and outright deflation plagued commodity markets.

In addition, stocks were about as buoyant as they have been in the 1980s. Even the insider trading scandals of the two eras have much in common.

The most striking parallel, however, may be between the economic position of the United States in the late 1920's and that of Japan today. In many ways, Japan is where the United States was 60 years ago, an emerging world economic power experiencing rapid growth amid a stagnant global economy.

This boom, however, has its drawbacks. Even though Japan is well off now, its rapid growth is creating internal imbalances and distortions that may turn its next recession into a disaster similar to that of the United States in the 1930's.

The United States, on the other hand, now is more like Great Britain in the 1920's and 1930's. After losing its world dominance after World War I, Britain suffered from slow growth, industrial over-capacity and high unemployment. Still, Britain did not take as big a fall as the United States during the Depression. So, if history repeats itself, this country's decline likewise might not be as severe in the next economic downturn.

Consider the historical similarities. Between the world wars, the United States blossomed into a world economic leader.

U.S. unemployment averaged only 3.7% between 1922 and 1929, and gross national product grew almost 40%. The trade surplus amounted to more than 1% of GNP, and the United States became a net international lender.

Money flowed into U.S. securities; stock prices rose 497% from 1921 to 1929. Meanwhile, the pound was overvalued because Britain went back to the prewar gold standard, and to prevent a capital flight to the United States, the U.S. Federal Reserve artificially held down interest rates. This encouraged stock investment at the expense of bonds and made borrowing to speculate in stocks attractive.

Then things came unglued. The Dow fell 89% between 1929 and 1932; the consumer price index declined 24% between 1929 and 1933, and GNP was off 22%. The ratio of the value of stocks on the New York Stock Exchange to GNP was cut in half between 1929 and 1931, to 35% from 70%.

In Britain, where speculation had been considerably less rampant and the market rise during the 1920's was only one-sixth of Wall Street's, the crash was not as severe.

Now America is the waning economic power and the waxing one is Japan. The United States has long been the high-cost producer in many industries, but this fact remained hidden during the shortages of the 1970's. Then the world took a turn to surpluses and competition intensified. The desire to consume and the inability to compete led to huge U.S. trade deficits that by 1986 reached 3.5% of GNP.

To finance our trade gap, we had to borrow, last year becoming a net international debtor for the first time since World War I. Unemployment remains above 6% despite 4 1/2 years of expansion and fiscal stimulus requiring annual budget deficits that have exceeded $200 billion.

Like the isolationist United States between the two world wars, Japan appears reluctant to accept the role of a dominant economic power. But even in a world of excess supply, Japan has amassed a phenomenal $100-billion trade surplus in the fiscal year ended March 31, up from $53 billion a year before.

The Japanese stock market has been extremely bullish. In a decade, Tokyo's share of world stock market trading has risen to 36% from 14%, while Wall Street's has fallen to 36% from 61%. Just as the United States held down its interest rates low to support the pound in the 1920's, Japan now is keeping interest rates low to support the dollar, encouraging investment in that nation's stocks.

The environment is ideal for 1920's-style speculation, which has been rampant. The ratio of stock market value to GNP in Japan is 130%, compared to 60% in the United States, Nippon Telegraph & Telephone, for example, has a price-to-earnings ratio of more than 250 and a market value exceeding that of the entire West German stock market.

Signs of trouble for the Japanese economy have surfaced, however. In the years following World War II, Japan was able to develop rapidly by imitating and adapting Western technology and becoming a low-cost producer of an increasingly sophisticated array of exports. But now the newly industrialized countries are following its footsteps.

Their success has been enviable; in 1970, Korea, Taiwan, Hong Kong, Singapore, Brazil and Mexico, accounted for just 4% of global exports; today they account for 10%, more than Japan does.

Thus far, Japan has been able to find even more sophisticated goods to stay ahead of the newly industrialized countries and maintain its export-led growth. Whether it can continue to do so isn't clear.

Moreover, the strong yen and protectionism are forcing many Japanese firms to produce abroad -- in the newly industrialized countries, Europe and North America. By the year 2000, Japan's largest manufacturing firms are expected to produce some 20% of their output abroad, compared to 3.4% in 1982.

Unemployment already has hit the postwar high of 3%. If the "hidden jobless" -- those who would be out of jobs if they didn't have guaranteed lifetime employment -- are taken into account, the rate certainly would be much higher. How long can these surplus workers be assigned to trim the hedge around the factory building?

The next recession, therefore, may bring the Japanese

economy down with a crash that will be spearheaded by the same sort of overheated stock market the United States experienced before the Great Depression. In the United States this time, the recession will be considerably milder, not because we are in an intrinsically stronger position but because our recent economic gains have been far smaller than Japan's, and the speculation in our markets has been far less rabid.

IV

AMERICA'S DWINDLING MIDDLE CLASS

(The Los Angeles Times, May 26, 1987.) After rising steadily since World War II, the nation's living standard stumbled in the 1970's and 1980's. Between 1973 and 1985, average real income per household fell 2%, and wage and salary income dropped nearly 10%.

Even more important, this decline was accompanied by income redistribution away from the middle class. The share of households with incomes over $50,000 or under $20,000 -- the rich and the poor -- rose 9% and 8%, respectively, and that of households in the middle dropped 9%.

Contrary to a common view, this wasn't due to changes in household structure. True, female-headed and non-family households grew sharply between 1973 and 1985, but their incomes also rose. In fact, their income distribution came to nearly mirror the national norm.

Nor did the rise of the two-earner family push many middle-income households up the income scale. In 1985, the biggest group of two-earner families made from $35,000 to $40,000 a year -- precisely the income range where the largest declines occurred. Apparently, families needed a second income just preserve their economic status, not to improve it.

The cause of the dwindling of the middle class -- and the key to income distribution patterns in the future -- is the changing labor market. Since 1973, jobs in high-paying occupations such as management, professional specialties and sales have constituted a rising share of private nonfarm employment, at the expense of moderate-paying occupations.

And since 1979, high-paying occupations have fared better against inflation than have moderate- and low-paying jobs, which have been victimized by foreign competition, deregulation and cost control.

At the same time, the share of jobs in middle-income employment categories, such as construction, manufacturing and transportation and public utilities, declined. Mining, where the energy crisis provided jobs, was the only exception among the middle-income industries.

Collectively, these categories went from accounting for 43.5% of all employment in 1973 to 39.2% in 1979 and to 33.2% by 1985. Meanwhile, the share of jobs grew in lower-paying categories such as wholesale and retail trade, finance, insurance and real estate and services.

The middle-income groups also were hit by the rise in the jobless rate from 4.0% in 1973 to 7.2% in 1985. In both years, about 15% of households experienced unemployment. But in 1985, the period of unemployment lasted longer, reducing incomes by 40%, compared to about 30% in 1973.

Another important development was the rise in part-time employees, especially involuntary ones (workers who would rather have full-time jobs), whose ranks swelled 127%. Part-time employment allows managers to lower labor costs and use workers more efficiently, but has a disastrous effect on incomes. Involuntary part-timers often are primary breadwinners, and the rapid growth of this group helps explain the increase in low-income households.

The 1973-1985 period began with low productivity and inflation, but ended with disinflation, global competition and, most importantly, cost control. These three features are likely to dominate the next decade as well, suggesting that belt-tightening has only begun.

Cost control is certain to spread from manufacturing to all sectors of the economy, and second- and third-generation organizational and staffing improvements will build upon the initial gains. While household incomes, spurred by higher productivity, probably will rise by around 1% a year during the next decade -- modestly by historical standards, but better than the average annual decline of 0.2% in the 1973-85 period -- income polarization is likely to intensify.

Management, professional and sales jobs probably will continue to grow more than other occupations, even if their own growth rate slows as managers themselves become targets of restructuring. The share of moderate-paying occupations will continue to dwindle, but also at a slower rate. As the U.S. trade deficit stabilizes, jobs will no longer flow abroad, but will be hurt by automation as U.S. business strives to regain its competitiveness.

Another factor enhancing U.S. competitiveness is pay moderation -- a trend dating back from the early 1980's, when management successfully challenged organized labor, capping wage settlements and reducing power.

In the next decade, pay moderation should not only endure but spill over to non-union jobs.

In contrast, the pay gains of the higher-paying jobs are likely to widen; firms will be willing to pay more for quality managers, who are indispensible in a highly competitive environment.

Upper-income households also should benefit disproportionately from gains in ownership income (business, investment or interest income), which in coming years is expected to rise much faster than wages and salaries.

The overall effect of these trends likely will be a substantial increase in the number of households with annual incomes between $5,000 and $20,000 in 1985 dollars, as well as those with incomes of $60,000 or more. The number of middle-income households will decline commensurately; most will be forced into the lower-income range, although a few will move up.

Unlike the past decade, the percentage of households in the $50,000-$60,000 range also will fall significantly, mainly because many middle-management jobs will be eliminated. At the same time, the gains in households with incomes over $60,000, aided by rising ownership income, will be dramatic.

The 1973-85 period saw the transition from shortages to surpluses and from high inflation to disinflation. In the next decade, disinflation, which has the strongest impact on income polarization, should be felt in full.

The projections portend significant change in the living standards of many American households. The scale of these changes will have major implications for national spending and savings patterns and will affect a wide range of social, political and economic issues. For example, many Americans who find themselves irrevocably sliding down from the ranks of the middle class may vent their frustration on imports, lending support for severe protectionist measures now brewing in Congress.

V

DISPOSSESSING THE NEXT GENERATION

(The Wall Street Journal, June 1, 1987.) It's been obvious for years that Americans save far too little. Ever since the New Deal, we've become more and more a nation of consumers. But there's no such thing as a free lunch. What we spend now is borrowed from the next generation.

Congress has finally begun to understand that excess consumption comes at the expense of tomorrow. Last year's tax revision made a number of changes to discourage borrowing, in particular phasing out the deductibility of interest on consumer loans. But the job is still incomplete.

The administration considered including mortgage interest in the phase-out, but the real estate interests rallied, and consequently, mortgage interest on first and even second homes remains tax deductible with few limitations. Moreover, the deductibility extends to home equity loans and second mortgages.

Is this just? Sure, home ownership ranks with motherhood and apple pie in most Americans' eyes, but is it fair that one group of consumers -- homeowners with mortgages -- is subsidized by the tax system, while other groups are not? One of the key objectives of last year's tax reform was to create fairness and neutrality in the tax code, but the new law rewards those with home equity that can be converted into borrowing.

Another question is: Has the new tax law served the purpose of discouraging borrowing? Clearly not.

Excrutiating Pressure

Because it has lagged behind the rest of the world in productivity growth, U.S. business is now cutting costs vigorously for the first time since the 1930's. But in a world of surpluses, cost cutting almost inevitably results in squeezes on incomes. As a result, the purchasing power of many middle-income Americans, both blue- and white-collar workers, is under excruciating pressure.

Since most Americans believe that their birthright includes living higher on the hog than their parents did and retiring rich, they are unwilling to face the fact that the American dream of ever-increasing purchasing power is gone for them, and that they've got to learn to live on less. Many are borrowing heavily to finance lifestyles they can't afford but are unwilling to give up.

Despite the new tax law, consumers are still borrowing. They've simply turned away from installment loans to second mortgages to finance cars, appliances, vacations and a variety of non-housing-related expenditures. Indeed, according to a Federal Reserve survey, home-equity loans as a share of mortgages outstanding on single-family houses rose to 10.8% in the fourth quarter of 1986 from 9% in the third quarter. That is a jump of $35 billion in just three months. The survey also found that only one-third of home-equity loans are used to buy or improve real estate.

(Cutbacks in federal student loan programs have also encouraged consumer borrowing, particularly in the form of second mortgages, since interest on student loans in other forms is no longer fully deductible.)

Many lenders are making borrowing on second mortgages very easy. The borrower is given a revolving line of credit against the previously unencumbered equity in his house, and he can draw against this credit line with a credit card. Borrowers have responded to these inducements with zeal.

It was, of course, during the closing months of last year that Congress passed the new tax law, which restricted interest rate deductibility outside of home mortgages. Second mortgages outstanding now equal about $180 billion, up from only $20 billion in 1981.

There's lots more borrowing power still available. In the 1970's, inflation pushed new housing prices up 33% faster than incomes advanced, and provided a tremendous pool of equity that homeowners are tapping for all sorts of spending. Even if homeowners retain an average of 20% unencumbered equity in their houses, they could still withdraw more than $1 trillion.

Government-subsidized second mortgages, applied to this huge pool of home equity, will give new life to reckless borrowing. Installment debt already has reached a record level of almost 20% of disposable personal income, and now consumers have a new source of credit to tap into. The problem, however, is that by liquidating the remaining unencumbered equity in their houses, homeowners won't have it to pass on to their children, who consequently will not be able to afford to buy the houses they grew up in.

In other words, those who already own houses that have appreciated greatly since they bought them may be able to live the good life they can't otherwise afford by tapping into that appreciation. But unless another round of serious inflation in house pricing occurs, which is unlikely, their children will not be able to repeat the exercise.

Furthermore, many people are paying for their children's college educations by taking out second mortgages. Once that equity is liquidated, there will be nothing left to pay for their children's educations.

Homeowners may come to their senses and reduce their second mortgage borrowing. But if recent trends continue, the consequences will be significant and disruptive:

> The U.S. will again become largely a nation of renters, as was the case prior to World War II. In 1930, 47.8% of American housing units were owner-occupied. The percentage grew with the postwar housing boom and easy homeowner financing to reach 65.8% in 1980. More recently, however, the ratio has begun to slip, falling to 63.9% at the end of 1986.

With houses less affordable, multi-generational households will continue to grow rapidly. It is already common, even in affluent suburbs, for college graduates to live at home for at least several years of their initial working lives. Between 1980 and 1985, the percentage of men aged 18 to 24 still living in their parents' homes has risen to 60% from 54%. For women, the percentage rose to 48% from 43%.

. Unable to afford their own homes, more people will live in rented houses or apartments, leading to higher rents and more active apartment construction after the current glut is absorbed.

. The prices of single-family houses will fall toward affordable levels, but this will further reduce ownership equity. Moreover, many parents now lend down-payment funds to their children -- often using their own homes as collateral. But if parents' equity is reduced, the children will not be able to afford houses of their own, even at lower prices, so a downward spiral in housing prices could result.

. The high cost of college education will come under pressure, since parents will no longer have the equity in their houses to pay their children's tuition bills.

Full Circle

. Saving rates probably will rise substantially. One of the reasons given for the extraordinarily high saving rate in Japan is the extremely high cost of housing. The average Japanese saves about 22% of his income and even then can't accumulate enough to buy a house until he's in his mid-50's. With Americans now saving an average of only 4% of their take-home pay, the potential for increases in saving are huge.

We've come then, full circle. The continuing deductibility of interest on home mortgages may will lead eventually to an increase in consumer saving. In the process,
the next generation will be disinherited and unable to
afford the houses they grew up in. It's too bad Washington didn't end the tax subsidy for mortgage interest last
year and thereby encourage saving. The alternative way
of getting to the same result may be painful and
disruptive.

VI

BANKS WISE TO BITE BULLET ON LOANS

(Los Angeles Times, July 21, 1987.) The decision by the
major banks to increase their reserves for possible losses
on loans to developing countries was based on a number of
very sound reasons. It has become painfully clear that the
money borrowed by developing nations in the 1970s, when
the prices of their commodity exports were soaring and
inflation-adjusted interest rates were very low, was not
put to productive use.

Much of it has been squandered on useless or unprofitable projects or smuggled into Swiss bank accounts. In
the 1980's most commodity prices have collapsed, and real
interest rates have risen to very high levels, so the chance
of those loans being serviced -- much less repaid in full --
are small.

By increasing reserves, the banks simply were admitting a painful reality that the markets in which those
loans trade realized long ago -- developing country loans
sell at discounts of about 40%. Stock investors, too, see
developing country loans as dead weight on the banks'
books. This explains why stocks of regional banks generally outperform those of the big money center banks with
heavy Third World exposure. By reserving, executives of
the banks simply caught up with their shareholders.

Except for a handful of financially weak banks, the
stock market welcomed the banks' decision, and their
shares rose. Indeed, additional reserves will strengthen
the banks' hand in dealing with debtors. Before, debtors

could blackmail banks by threatening to suspend payments and devastate their earnings. It's been said often enough that if you owe the bank $1,000 and can't pay, it's your problem, but if you owe $10 million and can't pay, it's the bank's problem. Now, the banks' vulnerability to such tactics is greatly reduced.

The implications of the banks' action are profound:

- The Federal Reserve under its chairman, Paul Volcker, has long been aware that many of those loans are uncollectible. The Fed has done every-thing to extend the business expansion to give banks breathing space in which to build up their capital and cushion themselves against developing country loans. Taking additional reserves abruptly ends the period in which the bankers kept rolling over loans to avoid facing reality. As they say in the financial community, "A rolling loan gathers no loss."

- Regional banks have long been unhappy with devel-oping country lending. Last year, they balked at providing their share of new money to bail out Mexico after the oil price collapse. Now, they may decide to write off all developing country loans an exit the scene. The debtors would then face only a handful of money center banks, whose negotiating stance would be toughened following the boost to their reserves. Debtors could conclude that they have little to gain from being cooperative.

- Increased reserves and writeoffs will reveal more clearly the quality differences among banks. Win-ners will include a number of regional banks that have boosted their reserves not only against inter-national loans but against questionable domestic loans as well. Foreign banks also would benefit. They didn't plunge head-on into developing country lending in the 1970s and have long reserved fully against the loans they made. Moreover, European and Japanese banks can afford to worry less about the possibility of writing off developing country loans now that the dollar has weakened against their currencies. Most of those loans are in dollars, and are worth less in terms of deutsche marks, yen, and other strong currencies. Losers will include money center banks with weakened capital positions and enormous foreign debt exposure.

Even after the latest boost, the banks' reserves probably are inadequate. Developing country loans trade at 60% of their face value, but even those prices may be inflated. Most transactions are conducted among the banks themselves, with few outside buyers and little new money coming in.

At the same time, debt-for-equity swaps, which have lately been touted as a potential solution to the debt crisis, assume that there is enough equity in developing countries worthy of serious investment. Once the banks start swapping their loans for equity on a larger scale, they may find that there isn't, and there will suddenly be too many dollars chasing too few sound investment opportunities. Already, discounts in debt-for-equity swaps are widening.

The banks' decision probably will drive the last nail into the coffin of Treasury Secretary James Baker's plan to provide new private funds to major debtor nations in exchange for promises to restructure their economies and develop their export industries. Most of those nations lack the zeal or the ability to revamp their inefficient economies, and the banks' action is, in effect, a resounding vote of no confidence in debtors' economic programs. It seems that only heavy pressure from the federal government could induce private banks to provide additional funds. It is, apparently, precisely this kind of U.S. government pressure that make a success of Argentina's recent debt refinancing campaign.

In short, the likelihood of more developing countries following Peru, Ecuador and Brazil into default has increased, while at the same time reserves taken by the banks are insufficient to shield them against the consequences. The U.S. government may in the end be forced to bail the banks out by taking over the loans directly. Yet, the effect of this action on the budget deficit may be unacceptable -- as would be the political reaction.

Is there a realistic solution to the debt problem? A panacea may never be found, but, in combination, several measures may defuse the time bomb. Debt-for-equity swaps are reducing the debt burden somewhat, and additional measures may include changing import quotas in favor of goods from the big debtor nations, reducing interest rates on selected loans and changing accounting rules to allow orderly writeoffs of uncollectible loans over a long period, perhaps 40 or 50 years.

In the meantime, the road is likely to be rocky. In particular, since so many debtor nations rely on U.S. markets to earn the hard currency they need to service their debts, the next U.S. recession, whenever it comes -- and the concomitant reduction in U.S. appetite for imports -- will test debtors' ability to stay solvent.

VII

SURPLUS, NOT SHORTAGE, IS NOW THE RULE

(The New York Times, August 30, 1987.) Fighting the last war is a favorite sport in business and financial circles, and today that war is the shortages and near-runaway inflation of the 1970's. The decline in the unemployment rate to 6 percent in July for the first time since 1979 has started yet another battle in that war -- fear that the foreign trade balance will improve so rapidly that labor supplies and industrial capacity will be strained.

In contrast we remain convinced that we're in a world of surpluses of almost everything for the first time since the 1930s. My recent book, The World Has Definitely Changed: New Economic Forces and Their Implications for the Next Decade, makes the case for global surpluses continuing for at least a decade. How does this apply here?

To begin, recent statistics show that while deterioration in the trade balance has stopped, rapid evaporation of the huge deficit is unlikely -- despite the weak dollar and efforts by American business to cut costs and regain competitiveness. This is not surprising in a world of excess capacity, and in strong-currency countries, producers are cutting costs and shifting production to the much lower-cost newly industrialized countries, or NIC's, to avoid price hikes in dollar terms and loss of their markets in the United States.

Furthermore, American economic growth is shifting toward industries with ample supplies of men and machines. Earlier rapid growth in financial and other services, military spending and housing created white-hot East and West Coast economies. In between lay the vast depression belt in which agriculture and energy industries were collapsing, and manufacturing was being decimated by surging imports.

More recently, coastal activity has cooled while the heartland has revived. The trade balance isn't improving enough to push manufacturing activity through the roof, but at least American goods, production and consumption are growing in step.

Economic growth, then, has moved toward manufacturing, where productive resources have been made plentiful by foreign competition and the cost-cutting response by American business. Since 1978, steel industry employment has declined by over 50 percent, electrical equipment by 25 percent and autos and metal-working machinery by 15 percent.

The shift from nonmanufacturing to manufacturing is also a shift from low- to high-productivity growth sectors. Consequently, much more output growth can be handled without straining labor supplies. From 1980 to 1986, manufacturing output per manhour grew 4 percent a year as cost control and restructuring became dominant corporate activities, while nonmanufacturing productivity grew a pitiful four-tenths of 1 percent a year. The recent acceleration in manufacturing activity will heighten productive growth further, as overhead is spread over more units of output.

In fact, the shift plus the increasing pressure on nonmanufacturing to control costs should lead to economywide productivity growth of 2.5 percent annually in coming years. Combining this with our forecast real G.N.P. growth of 3 percent means that demand for manhours will rise only five-tenths of 1 percent a year. Thank goodness labor force growth is slowing. Otherwise, we would be facing massive unemployment

Also, a return to rapid wage increases is unlikely. In today's world of fierce competition, American businessmen are no longer paternalistic, but are determined to make a reasonable profit, even closing operations if necessary. Most employees accept this, and are more interested in job security than pay hikes that may be followed by layoffs.

In fact, the squeeze on wages by cost-cutting businessmen has been so great that increases have fallen short of inflation for many middle-income families. They don't want to give up the American dream of ever-higher living standards, so they borrow to maintain lifestyles they can't afford.

Consequently, the nation faces a depressing dilemma. If wages and fringe benefits rise enough to increase purchasing power meaningfully, American business will again be priced out of the markets at home and abroad and economic activity will decline. But if labor and other cost cuts continue, purchasing power will remain depressed, and once consumers cease their excessive borrowing, the economy will falter.

Strains on industrial capacity should also continue to be few. Utilization rates are far below the 1970's peaks, even after adjusting for obsolete facilities that are still on the books, on the one hand, and the more intense utilization of remaining plant and equipment, on the other. Furthermore, export capacity in the NIC's continues to mushroom. Several industries, notably paper and some chemical industry segments, have experienced supply constraints, but recently, some paper companies have announced huge capacity additions.

Finally, even in the remote, highly unlikely possibility that we're dead wrong and instead, the foreign trade sector surges and somehow strains labor and industrial capacity, significant inflation is still unlikely. Those who are fighting the last war of inflation in the 1970's would undoubtedly anticipate renewed trouble and push up interest rates to the point of precipitating a recession that would remove those strains quickly.

This brings us back to the beginning. Fighting the last war is aiming at the wrong target, but it probably prevents that war from recurring. Unfortunately, it also prevents serious focussing on the next war, the logical implication of the excess supply world -- deflation, widespread financial crises and protectionism Given the possible severity of that war, it deserves a lot more attention that it's getting.

VIII

CAN CONSUMERS SUSTAIN GROWTH?

(The Los Angeles Times, September 15, 1987) Since mid-1984, real gross national product has been increasing at a 3% annual rate -- just about the long-term trend. It is very modest, however, compared to the 7% average annual growth rate in the opening stages in this expansion -- from late 1982 through the first half of 1984. An occasional quarter during this slow-growth period has been robust but on balance, it has been a monotonous and sluggish performance.

In the most recent quarters, however, the growth pattern has changed. In the early part of the slow-growth period, the consumer was the driving force in the economy. In 1986 alone, consumer spending grew 5.4% in real terms, and durable goods spending surged 11.5%.

But in the first six months of this year, consumers slowed down: Consumer spending grew at an annual rate of only 0.9%, and durables purchases fell at an annual rate of 5.2%. Consumption contributed only 14% to the rise in GNP in the most recent quarter.

But, just as the consumer faltered, a new source of economic growth emerged, spearheaded by a foreign sector rebound. A combination of the weak dollar, cost control by U.S. business and restructuring at many U.S. companies has finally halted the worsening of our trade deficit. In inflation-adjusted terms, imports have leveled off while exports have risen, posting a particularly impressive gain in the latest quarter, despite some recent setbacks. A wide variety of exports, including industrial supplies and materials, capital goods and even agricultural products, has shown strength.

I remain convinced that, in a world of surpluses, further reductions in our trade deficit are likely to be painfully slow. Nevertheless, even the end of the decline in the trade balance would be a boost to the economy -- the removal of a negative force becomes a positive factor.

The economy, then, is in a period of consumer slowdown but, at the same time, it is experiencing an end, and possibly a reversal, of the decline of the trade balance, especially due to export strength. Overall, GNP growth is likely to remain modest -- perhaps in the 2% to 2.5% range -- but the economy is now much better balanced.

Earlier, robust consumer spending did not translate into strength in manufacturing, because virtually all the increase in goods consumed in this country came from abroad. Until last fall, U.S. industrial production grew very slowly -- less than 1% per year over two years.

This weakness, of course, was a direct counterpart of the strength in imports, which gave rise to a unique situation: The ratio of industrial production to GNP actually declined during a business expansion. Normally, the ratio falls in recessions, when consumers postpone purchases of durable goods, forcing businesses to cut inventories and capital spending. In this recovery, however, for the first time in the postwar period, the ratio declined even as consumption growth remained strong.

Starting the second half of last year, the flattening in imports and growth in exports have spurred a rise in U.S. industrial production that has matched the growth in the overall economy. Now, American goods consumption and production are growing in step, and the ratio of industrial production to GNP has flattened.

The switch to a more balanced growth in goods and consumption has important geographic ramifications. Earlier, the U.S. economy was described as bicoastal: Consumer spending spurred growth on the East and West coasts, while a vast depression belt consisting of weak manufacturing and collapsed agriculture and energy sectors lay in between. Now, activity on the coasts has cooled off, with slower consumer spending growth. But the pickup in manufacturing, as well as the modest revival in the agricultural and energy sectors, have breathed some life into the heartland.

But is a better balanced economy sustainable? Consumers, even at slower rates of consumption, are still sinking deeper and deeper into hock and drawing down their remaining assets, including the equity in their homes. The reason for this is that while spending growth slowed, purchasing power actually fell in the first half of 1987.

Nominal income growth has long been extremely weak; recently, however, an uptick in inflation has turned modest gains into losses in real terms. In the first quarter, hourly compensation in the non-farm sector rose at 1.1% rate in nominal terms, but fell at a 3.9% rate when adjusted for inflation. In the second quarter, the nominal growth rate of 2.9% translated into a 1.9% rate of decline for purchasing power.

The revival in manufacturing, as indicated earlier, has largely been the result of uncompromising cost-control efforts by U.S. business. this is the most exciting development in my business career. It will, I believe, restore our international competitiveness and push operating earnings up at a compounded rate of 9% to 10% during the next decade. But the obverse of cost control is a squeeze on incomes.

The effects of cost control on middle-income households have been, and will probably continue to be, devastating. Households with pretax incomes in the $20,000 to $60,000 range in 1985 dollars -- the core of the American middle-class -- saw their share of total households fall from 53% in 1973 to 49% in 1985, and will probably drop to 38% by 1995.

Thus far, consumers have been supplementing the shortfall in their incomes by borrowing. Sooner or later, however, they'll have to pull in their horns. In the past three years, consumers have been able to carry the economy virtually single-handedly. Can manufacturing do the same when they stop? Consumer spending accounts for roughly two-thirds of the economy. Moreover, as indicated earlier, further solid gains for U.S. manufacturing at the expense of foreign producers won't be easy.

Moreover, the United States has been the only locomotive in this recovery. Many foreign economies, including those of most Western European nations and Japan, rely on their sales in this country to generate growth. If U.S. consumers sharply reduced their spending, our trading partners would themselves plunge into a recession, throttling the nascent revival in our exports.

IX

CONSUMERS TO GET RUDE AWAKENING
FROM AMERICAN DREAM

(Los Angeles Times, November 22, 1987.) The stock market crash may have profound effects not only on stock investors but also on consumers, the vast majority of whom own no stocks. It may well be the long-awaited rude shock that will awaken the middle class to the fact that the American Dream is long over for them and force them to change their spending patterns. The implications for the business and economic environment are dramatic.

The American Dream has always meant ever-rising living standards and even higher incomes for our kids. But for many Americans this is no longer the case, because of the world of surpluses that we are facing for the first time since the 1930s. The flood of foreign exports, not just from Europe and Japan but from South Korea, Taiwan, and other newly industrialized countries, has pushed the yearly U.S. merchandise trade deficit close to $200 billion. U.S. business has reacted to heightened competition by cutting costs: High-paying jobs are being eliminated, benefits pared and production moved from union facilities in the North to the low-cost Sun Belt or even abroad.

U.S. wages for low-skilled jobs in basic industry are not competitive with those in the newly industrialized countries, to which production is increasingly fleeing. Unit labor costs in manufacturing are 10 times higher here than in South Korea and eight times higher here than in Taiwan. The fall in the dollar needed to close this gap is not only astronomical but almost impossible: a hotel room in Seoul would then cost more than $1,000 a night!

More Non-Union Workers

Worse still, many unionized industries are not even competitive at home. Such industries as steel and autos pay their workers as much as two-thirds more than what non-unionized Americans with similar skills are willing to work for. No wonder employment is shifting to non-union workers: In the non-farm work force, the share of unionized workers fell from 30% in 1955 to 16% in 1986.

In every major sector, weekly wages for non-supervisory workers peaked in 1973 or 1979 and have declined since then.

In some sectors, such as retailing, they have fallen sharply in the 1980s, largely due to heavy reliance by employers on part-time workers.

Indeed, part-timers can be scheduled to work only when needed, and additional cost savings can be gained since employers pay them fewer fringe benefits. Between 1973 and 1986 the number of involuntary part-time workers rose from 2.3 million to 5.3 million.

An employment shift is also under way from high-to low-paying industries, as a consequence of job losses to imports in many high-paying basic industries. Non-supervisory jobs in manufacturing fell from 28.4% of the total in 1973 to 19.3% in 1986, while retail employment rose from 21.4% to 23.7%, and service jobs from 22.2% to 30%. Yet manufacturing jobs pay half again as much as service jobs, and more than twice as much as retailing.

These developments, all closely related to fierce cost-cutting by U.S. business, caused real income per household to fall considerably in this decade.

Concentrating on wages and salaries alone -- the income mainstay for the overwhelming majority of ordinary consumers -- we see sharp declines in purchasing power. On balance, real wages and salaries per household dropped 8.7% from 1973 to 1986. And, after increasing earlier in this recovery, they dipped once again in the first half of this year. The share of households with $20,000 to $60,000 pretax incomes in 1985 dollars, the core of the middle class, slid from 53% of the total in 1973 to 49% in 1985.

As cost control accelerates, the share of this middle-income group will probably fall even more, to 38% by 1995. As those families' purchasing power is reduced, households with incomes below $20,000 in 1985 dollars are expected to rise to 50% of the total in 1995, compared to 39% in 1973.

Those on top, conversely, will continue to grow in number and income. Postwar babies are entering their top earning ages, and well-paid jobs for highly trained professionals are expanding in areas where the United States can compete internationally. The average income for households with pretax incomes over $60,000 in 1985 dollars, rose from $124,000 in 1973 to $135,000 in 1985 and is likely to reach $149,000 by 1995. Their share of total income will rise from 30% in 1973 to 50% in 1995.

Shrinking Families

Even though the decline in living standards for many began as long ago as the mid-1970s, most middle-income families have been slow to accept the fact that they can no longer live higher on the hog than their parents, or retire rich.

For a time, they have been able to delude themselves: First, in the 1970s, older women joined the work force, but that didn't prevent further erosions of household purchasing power. Then, those women postponed having children and had fewer of them: The average family size shrank from 3.42 in 1975 to 3.23 in 1985. That didn't work either. And now, people are borrowing to finance lifestyles that they can't afford but hate to give up.

Yet this borrowing can't go on forever. Sooner or later, people must face up to reality, which for them is the end of the American Dream They may do so now, with the stock market crash making them worry about a rerun of the Great Depression and revealing to them how financially overexposed they are.

The consequences will be enormous. First, the realization that the American Dream is over for them will lead to frustration, which might easily be vented through protectionism. "Cut those slave-labor-produced goods off at the border," they'll reason," and then we can return to the lifestyles we knew and loved."

Of course, protectionism doesn't work. Major actions to limit U.S. imports would trigger retaliation abroad, and everyone's trade and economic activity would suffer.

Second, income and spending shifts will cause changes in the markets for goods and services, as well as savings and investment flows.

Retailers serving top earners will continue to gain, as will those selling to low-income groups, but middle-market retailers will be squeezed along with their customers. Financial and other services favored by upper-income people will be big winners.

Third, the concentrating of income at the top will greatly increase savings and hence the fund for investment. In this country there is a clear division of labor between saving and spending: families with over $75,000 in pretax income save 38% of their after-tax dollars, but those with less than $10,000 in income spend $1.97 for every one of their after-tax dollars!

The income shift in favor of the upper-income households, coupled with demographic factors such as the natural aging of the U.S. population, should raise the saving rate from 5.1% in 1985 to more than 10% in 1995, a level that has been rare in the postwar era.

Finally, if as we expect, consumers pull in their spending horns as a result of the shock of the stock market crash and admit that the American Dream is over for many of them a recession will develop quickly.

Consumers account for two-thirds of GNP, so spending

restraint will drag down the whole economy. And the recession, which will probably start early in the new year, could be long and deep if it spawns severe protectionist legislation here and abroad, and financial crises that the Federal Reserve and other monetary authorities cannot contain.

The stock market crash will probably force many families to realize that the American Dream of ever increasing purchasing power is over for them. This will be a rude awakening to them, to those from whom they buy, and to those who will feel the effects of their frustrations.